SOCRATIC
SELLING SKILLS

The Discipline
of Customer-Centered Sales

by
KEVIN DALEY

in conjunction with
Communispond
www.communispond.com

Routledge
Taylor & Francis Group

NEW YORK AND LONDON

First published 2005 by Routledge
270 Madison Ave, New York, NY 10016

Routledge is an imprint of the Taylor & Francis Group

© 2005 IIR-Communispond, Inc.
www.communispond.com

British Library Cataloguing in Publication Data
Applied for

ISBN 0415 399726

Trademarks and service marks are the property of their owners.

CONTENTS

A Note on Style

An outmoded rule of English usage requires the masculine form of a pronoun (he, him, his) when the antecedent could be either gender. But this implies something about the relative status of genders that doesn't deserve support in this book. The logical way to make the language more gender-equitable is to replace "he" with "he or she." Replacing one word with three, however, is inelegant and often awkward. Our solution has been to use the feminine form sometimes and the masculine form other times. If the change from one to the other sometimes seems abrupt, we hope you nevertheless prefer it to the reinforcement of aging (and dying, we hope) stereotypes.

Foreword:

In the twenty years or so since we first developed the Socratic Selling Skills program, it has changed in various ways. We have added units on planning and strategy; we have tweaked it here and there. And it will probably change ever more as time goes by.

But the basic character of the program will never change. Its goal will always be to put the customer at the center of the sales process. It will always try to foster dialogue that uncovers information about customer needs and motivations.

When Communispond teaches Socratic Selling Skills, we usually run an intensive two-day seminar to teach the behaviors the salesperson needs to master. At the end of the first day, we always suggest to the participants that they try out one of their Socratic techniques that evening before they return the next day. It doesn't have to be a selling situation. It can be a conversation at home with a spouse. It can be a dialogue about anything with anybody.

The results are always a little miraculous. Everyone has a story about a success in drawing someone out. We've had people learn new things about family members they thought they knew very well. We've had parents who got teenagers to talk about their own lives at the dinner table. We even had a student once who went to see a customer about certain details of current arrangements and reported in the seminar the next day that he'd secured a commitment for a whole new line of business.

We have seen over the years that the skills of Socratic Selling are more than a way to quickly establish customer relationships and close sales predictably, they are a way of life.

The truth is that most people are rarely listened to. When you have mastered the skills of listening and you make the effort to apply them in your relationships (personal as well as professional), the results are invariably spectacular. Socratic Selling Skills, in other words, connect you to the people you interact with. They don't just make you a better salesperson. They make you a better (and more fulfilled) human being.

Many Communispond employees, and even participants in our seminars and classes, have contributed to the development and refinement of Socratic Selling Skills. We could never hope to name them all. But we can name the Communispond employees who particularly contributed to this book by sharing their thoughts and experiences. We want to thank Allan Berger, Jeanie Bress, Bill Lusk, and Jack Swanson—Socratic salespeople all—for the time and thought they invested in the project.

In addition, three Communispond customers—Rich Bigger, Director of Training and Customer Relations for the Higher Education Division of John Wylie Publishing; James Brown, Director of Marketing Strategy for Shell Trading Gas & Power; and Ann Martin, Director of Sales Training for Wyndham International—were generous with their experiences and opinions. They are all strong supporters of Socratic Selling Skills, and we want to thank them.

A book like this can never be more than an introduction to a discipline like Socratic Selling Skills. You won't know how dramatically these skills can change your life until you practice them. I urge you to try some of the things you read about in this book to see if they don't make both your professional and personal lives more prosperous and fulfilling. After you've tried them, come visit us on the web at www.communispond.com. We would love to know how they worked for you.

Kevin Daley
Communispond
52 Vanderbilt Avenue
New York, NY 10017

Prologue:

ANCIENT GREEKS AND MODERN SELLING

In the twenty years since we first developed Socratic Selling, a number of people have questioned our choice of Socrates as the patron saint of sales. Socrates himself was not by any stretch of the imagination a successful salesman. And from what little we know of his life today, his conduct was anything but salesman-like.

Socrates was a philosopher, but he was unusual by today's standards in that he never wrote anything. The medium by which he communicated his philosophy was his own life. He didn't write about his beliefs. He lived them.

Born in Athens in the second half of the fifth century B.C. (some say 469, but the actual year is uncertain), he was the son of a stonemason and a midwife. He grew up in prosperous circumstances. We know this because he served in the infantry in the Peloponnesian War, and infantrymen were required to furnish their own armor and weaponry.

He is said to have learned to endure hardship during his military service. You might even think he acquired a taste for it, because in his later years he was well known for wearing thin, inadequate clothing in the harshest weather and for going barefoot even though he could easily afford shoes. Dressing absent-mindedly and going barefoot were not his only shortcomings. He talked incessantly. This picture of Socrates as a man who ignored fashion and talked too much comes down to us from comic sketches and plays. Apparently, making fun of Socrates and his habits was a pastime among Athenian writers.

The ridicule was not good-natured, however. Socrates was widely disliked. He was a threat to the conservative elements of Athenian society. A skeptic, his principal occupation was the questioning of people's religious, scientific, and moral beliefs. His questioning went particularly hard on you if you were pretentious. An argument with Socrates (for his conversation consisted almost entirely of argument) left a person feeling chastened, if not humiliated.

In questioning the nature and premises of people's beliefs, Socrates was demanding that they live up to those beliefs. And people can only take so much of that. Finally, when Socrates was seventy, three men brought an indictment against him. The indictment was for failing to recognize the city's official gods and for corrupting the city's youth. Socrates was tried before a jury of 500 Athenian citizens. No actual record of the trial survives. The charge must have been difficult to beat, however, because so many Athenians had experienced Socrates' questioning of their religious beliefs. He had already proved himself irreligious in the eyes of many, and that attitude spoke directly to the charges of not recognizing the gods.

At his trial, Socrates employed an unusual self-defense. Although he forced his accusers to admit that he had educated youth rather than corrupting them, he didn't address the charges directly but instead took the opportunity to defend his way of life. Socrates may have correctly diagnosed the situation when he implied that he was being prosecuted for not living the way other people did, but eccentricity has never been a good defense strategy in a trial. A narrow majority of the jury found him guilty.

The city government was by this time embarrassed to be trying a famous philosopher, and in the penalty phase of the trial they asked Socrates to propose his own sentence. His first proposal was characteristically eccentric—free meals for life in the city hall. He suggested this, he said, because he considered himself a public benefactor. Eventually, however, his supporters, fearing the court's impatience, prevailed upon him to propose a fine equal to eight years' wages for a skilled laborer.

By that point, however, Socrates' eccentricity had thoroughly alienated the court. The court voted to execute him. The majority that voted for execution was larger than the majority that had found him guilty.

Because of religious holidays, the execution could not be carried out for a month. Socrates was kept in prison for that month, but the imprisonment was lax, and a stream of friends and supporters came and went from his cell. The authorities may well have wished he would escape, and it probably would have been easy for him to do so. But he refused. In the same way he had spent his life forcing people around him to live up to their beliefs, he practically forced the city to execute him. At the end of the month, he was required to drink ground-up hemlock. It's not as pleasant a way to die as Plato later made it out to be, but some might consider it better than his society's favored method of execution, a kind of crucifixion.

What does Socrates' life tell us about selling? We would never advise a sales professional to go barefoot, to argue with customers about their beliefs, or to talk incessantly. So Socrates, at first glance, might not seem to be a great role model for sales professionals. But his lasting fame is not based on his eccentricities. It is based on his uncompromising belief in learning through questioning. He never assumed he knew what other people were thinking, and he believed that asking questions of them was the best way to help them reach new understandings. He believed, in other words, that questioning people was the best way to serve them, for he had an abiding belief in the importance of serving others.

As we noted above, Socrates left no writings behind, and most of what we know about him comes from the writings of his student, Plato. Although Plato regarded Socrates as his teacher, the Socrates that emerges in Plato's works is not an authority figure. He is an inquirer. In Plato's accounts, Socrates actually denies that he is a teacher and insists he has no wisdom to impart to anyone.

Socrates' spirit of humility and his drive for understanding are probably best illustrated in one of his more famous quotations: "As for me, all I know is that I know nothing." It is this Socrates whom we commend to you as a model for your life and work. This Socrates approached life with humility and strove to bring understanding to others by asking them questions. And he made the world a better place.

Chapter 1

THE OBLIVIOUS
SALESPERSON

The film *Breaking Away* takes place in Bloomington, Indiana during the 1970s. It's the story of a boy who aspires to a career in bicycle racing. The boy is the son of a retired stonecutter, played by Paul Dooley, who owns a small used-car lot. The best thing you can say about him as a car salesman is that he's a good stonecutter. In an early scene in the film, Dooley gives a pitch-perfect performance of a character we think of as the Oblivious Salesperson.

> *A young man is looking at a red sports car.*
> *Dooley starts toward him, shouting, "It gets thirty miles to the gallon."*
> *The young man says nothing. He opens the car door.*
> *"Of course," Dooley adds as he nears the car, "the mileage you get may vary."*
> *The man says nothing and climbs into the driver's seat.*

"It's a beaut, right?" says Dooley.
The young man still says nothing and looks over
the instruments on the dashboard.
"Right," says Dooley.
The young man raises and lowers the sun visor.
"Boy, you sure know how to pick 'em."
The young man says nothing.
"Frankly, this is the best car on the lot."
The young man says nothing.
"Quality product!" Dooley slaps the hood of the car.
Dooley's monologue ends—mercifully—when
another character enters the scene and interrupts.

There's a lot of truth in great fiction, and this scene will be familiar to any customer who has lived through this sort of sales pitch. The Oblivious Salesperson is someone who declaims the virtues of the product and continues talking about these virtues without regard to the customer's response. In this model, selling is an endurance event. Success supposedly comes to the one who can keep talking no matter what. The stereotype is so well known and accepted that it makes Dooley's scene in the film compelling.

Breaking Away is more than twenty-five years old as we write this, and the world has changed a lot in that time. But talking at customers without regard to their response isn't now and has never been an effective sales tactic.

Still, people continue to believe that talking at the customer works. We see students express this belief in our Socratic Selling Skills course all the time. Many, perhaps even most, students begin our course with the belief that they can make a sale if only they can enumerate some magic number of features or benefits of the product. So they spend the precious time of the sales call talking, reciting point after point. When the prospect inevitably shows signs of resistance to these points, they talk louder!

The Agenda-Focused Sales Call

That's not to say that most salespeople are boorish or that they bumble around like Dooley's character in *Breaking Away*. You can see the same approach even in the smoothest characters. Does this situation look familiar?

The salesperson enters the customer's office. It is the first sales call for this account. She is carrying a sleeping laptop that holds a PowerPoint file. It's a beautifully designed, elegant twenty-five-slide presentation about her company and her product.

"I know I promised you a half hour," says the customer, *"but something has come up and I have to be across town. I can give you fifteen minutes."*

The salesperson knows the presentation takes at least twenty minutes, but she doesn't know if she'll be able to get into this office again. She smiles and says, *"That's fine."*

"Let me make it easy on you," says the customer. *"I just need to know three things about your product.*

One: How long would it take to roll it out to 376 users at a single site? Two: How well does it run in a multiplatform environment? Three: Can you modify the interface to give it the look and feel of our existing systems?"

The salesperson wakes up her laptop. "I'm glad you asked those questions," she says. "I think you'll find they are all answered in this presentation."

Let's stop this scene right there. What's wrong with this picture?

The problem is that the customer asked for specific pieces of information and the salesperson is preparing to answer with a canned presentation. "I'm glad you asked those questions" may sound like a smooth transition, but she is using it to cover the fact that she's not answering him. She's not dealing with his concerns; she's ticking off agenda items. An inexperienced customer will probably feel vaguely uncomfortable with this and not quite know why. An experienced one will have heard the I'm-glad-you-asked-that-question dodge before and will be thinking of ways to throw her out of the office.

It may or may not be true that the customer's questions will be answered by the sales presentation. Even if it is true, however, what has the salesperson signaled to the customer with her response? She has said, in effect, "We are going to do this my way." That's not the way she should treat a person from whom she's trying to secure a commitment for thousands or even hundreds of thousands of dollars.

Furthermore, by insisting on going through the canned presentation when she has only fifteen minutes to do it, she has left herself only two possible outcomes. The first is that she cuts the twenty-minute presentation to fifteen minutes, causing her to stumble through it as she decides on the fly which screens to show and which to skip. The second possible outcome—even worse—is that she doesn't cut the presentation and gives him the full twenty minutes, which alienates the customer—perhaps even badly enough to cause her to lose the account altogether.

And yet, the scene described above is enacted over and over again in offices every day—the salesperson who approaches the customer with an agenda, oblivious to the customer's needs or desires.

Preparation and Product Knowledge

Why do some salespeople behave this way? It is partly a lack of preparation. Some people think that rehearsing a presentation constitutes preparation. But a PowerPoint presentation, no matter how well rehearsed, does not constitute preparation.

Preparation means creating an effective plan or strategy. A successful general doesn't prepare a strategy by looking only at her own resources and capabilities. She has to look also at the resources and capabilities on the other side. She has to know the terrain and the obstacles surrounding the objective. She needs weather reports. With this information in hand, she makes a plan for attaining the objective. That doesn't mean she won't deviate from the plan. In fact, you could argue that there is more value to creating a strategy than to following it. Creating a strategy forces you to account for everything that can affect your effort and helps you to prepare for surprises.

When we describe the process of formulating a strategy, we are speaking metaphorically, of course. You probably don't need to check The Weather Channel before going on a sales call (although in some seasons and regions, it's probably a good idea). But you need to know business conditions. Why did our salesperson's customer have to be across town suddenly? There's not enough information in the scene we've given you to answer that question. But our salesperson should have been prepared. She should have known the customer's industry and company well enough to know what kinds of crises were likely. Arguably, her sales call should be part of the solution to the customer's crisis and not just another fifteen-minute distraction along the way to dealing with it.

Another reason salespeople behave this way lies in tradition. Over the last half century, sales professionals have had to learn more and more technical detail. A classic book on selling published in 1977 (Roger W. Seng, *The Skills of Selling* [Amacom]), for example, devoted its second chapter to the need for technical mastery with the title, "Product Knowledge—The Prime Source of Selling Skill."

This emphasis on product knowledge is understandable. After all, if a product isn't complex, you don't need a salesperson to sell it. And the salesperson needs to know more about the product than the customer does, right? But if the salesperson's training emphasizes the product's functions and capabilities instead of the principles of the sales process, then the salesperson tends to treat the sales call as a product knowledge dump.

We are not saying that product knowledge is unimportant. We are only saying that dispensing product knowledge is not a sales strategy.

The Six Steps

The recent product knowledge revolution isn't the only tradition that encourages agenda-focused sales calls. It's unclear to us where the model originated, but as long as anyone can remember, sales trainers have been teaching that there are six steps in the selling process:

1. preparation
2. opening
3. discovering information
4. presentation
5. overcoming objections
6. closing

This model is fine as far as it goes, and for someone who knows how to use it, it can be very useful. (We must say, however, that the phrase "overcoming objections" is utterly unproductive. It makes the customer appear as the adversary. If we were to rewrite the model, we would probably label step five "inviting objections.")

But the six-step model can cause big trouble. People (including some sales trainers and managers) sometimes misunderstand it and assume it is a model of the sales call rather than of the sales process. In reality, the six steps can take months to complete, depending on the product and the customer. In addition, because the steps are numbered, people believe they must occur in order. That's not true, and treating the six-step model as a set of directions for controlling a sales call will usually result—once again—in agenda-focused selling.

Another reason some salespeople don't listen to customers has to do with performance management. Centuries of sales history have demonstrated that there is a direct relationship between the number of calls made and the number of sales closed. Sales managers, wanting to give their salespeople all the support they can, will sometimes give them quotas for sales calls. This emphasis on quantity instead of quality tends to reinforce agenda-focused behavior.

We are not saying that call quotas have no place in the management of sales professionals. Some sales managers like call quotas because they offer a standard against which to measure success. But remember that in the end, the only measurement that counts is how many sales are closed. Give your people call quotas, but make sure they understand that the job is not making sales calls. The job is selling the product.

The Modern Customer

If talking at customers was not an effective sales tactic twenty-five years ago when *Breaking Away* was made, it's even less effective today. Think for a moment about the modern customer and the resources at her disposal. Today, if you're selling cars, your customer is likely to already know the car's dealer cost, its crash rating, and how many units are in the possession of surrounding dealers. If you're selling computers, the customer is likely to have already read about the machine's performance, compatibility, and ergonomic issues. If you're selling insurance, the customer is likely to already have three or four quotes from other insurers in hand.

And these are just consumers! If you sell to business customers, they are an order of magnitude better informed about your product and your competitors' products. When buying stuff is part of your job, failing to take advantage of information sources is dereliction of duty. And there is enough information at a customer's fingertips today to make her exceedingly well informed. Much of your "product knowledge dump" will be wasted on a customer who knows all about your product, including complaints about it that dissatisfied customers have posted on the Web.

So the salesperson is no longer the source of all information in the sales process. Now, add in the fact that everybody is under more time pressure than ever before, and you can see the forces that are at work during a sales call. Well informed customers plus increased time pressure equals reduced patience with agenda-focused salespeople.

Tearing Up the Agenda

It should be clear that oblivious talking and mentally ticking off numbered steps are not helpful in a sales effort. But, you may argue, how many ways are there to sell a car? What can a salesperson do besides approach the customer and begin describing the excellence of the product?

Let's see how that scene from *Breaking Away* might have played out if it were a scene about successful sales techniques.

> *A young man is looking at a red sports car.*
> *Dooley approaches him. "Hi."*
> *The young man smiles but says nothing. He opens the car door and climbs into the driver's seat.*
> *"What was it about this car that caught your interest?" says Dooley.*
> *The young man turns to Dooley from the instrument panel and shrugs. "It's red."*
> *Dooley watches the young man as he looks over the instruments on the dashboard. Finally he speaks. "What kind of driving do you normally do?"*
> *The young man raises and lowers the sun visor. "I commute to work, but mostly I just need to get around."*
> *"Who rides with you?"*
> *The young man looks up, somewhat surprised at the question. "My girlfriend sometimes. Mostly, it's just me."*

"What do you like most in a car?"
The young man climbs out of the car. "Power."
"I have several red cars with big engines. Would
you like to see them?"
The young man brightens. "OK."

In this new scene, Dooley's character hasn't made the sale yet, but he has maintained the young man's interest and positioned himself as a guide to the products available. This scene, of course, is just as fictional as the original scene, and we were able to make it come out the way we wanted. But we think that if you look at it closely, you will see Dooley's character overcoming realistic customer resistance. And we think you will detect the ring of authenticity.

In this scene, Dooley's character is using something like Socratic Selling, and that's the subject of this book. Before we get into the theory and techniques of Socratic Selling, however, we are going to look at the principles that make it work.

Chapter
2

THE PRINCIPLES OF SOCRATIC SELLING

S ocratic Selling is a discipline that uses active listening and effective questioning to discover customer needs so that the customer and the salesperson can work together to meet those needs. By its very nature, it puts the customer first in the selling process.

If you want to master the discipline, you need to put your agenda aside and focus on the customer and her needs. That means, of course, that you don't push the customer, but it also means you don't lead the customer. This can be difficult for some sales professionals to grasp because they are, after all, in the business of selling.

Traditionally, salespeople have been trained to attempt to close the sale early and often. The classic approach is the trial close:

"If I were able to show you right now a way you could _____ without changing _____, would we have a basis for doing business?"

The blanks are usually filled with quantified benefits, but you can put in whatever you think the customer might want:

- increase revenue by $150,000 without changing costs
- raise market share by twenty points without changing the product
- cut turnover in half without changing employee salaries

It sounds a lot like the used-car lot, doesn't it?

If I were able to show you right now a way you could drive away in this gorgeous red car without changing your current household budget, would we have a basis for doing business?

Customers hate that. In fact, they hate it so much that the pressurized close has given the sales profession a bad name. Many companies have even changed the titles of all their salespeople to avoid the bad association. They call them "Business Development Associates" or "Account Managers" or "Consultants." Could there be a more powerful sign that customers hate the selling process?

Socratic Selling changes this by moving the focus from the salesperson to the customer. That change in focus is embodied in the nine principles of Socratic Selling:

Principle #1. To sell is to serve.

The idea of sales-as-service is at odds with the concept of the "aggressive salesperson" we all know so well from the want ads. Organizations want their sales professionals to "overcome objections" and "close the deal." Sometimes they will even use military metaphors, ordering their salespeople to "take no prisoners." In the hands of such organizations, the customer is a recalcitrant resource, like a cow that doesn't want to be milked.

The Socratic sales professional, on the other hand, adopts the goal of making the customer's life better. It's true that this goal generally results in a lasting relationship with the customer and a much more predictable close than occurs in traditional selling. But the goal is to serve the customer. That can sometimes mean not selling the product when it's not a good fit. It can even mean referring the customer to a different product. These are painful situations, to be sure, but if you can't make the customer's life better by selling her your product, your time is better spent elsewhere.

Socratic selling is about building permanent relationships. This focus, interestingly enough, tends to give sales professionals more confidence about approaching customers. They know they intend to make the customer's life better, and the sales process becomes almost a gift to the customer.

Don't scoff. One of our sales professionals was once referred to a new client by a long-time one. After he met with the new client, she telephoned the long-time client to explain how the meeting went. "He's my new best friend," she said. "Get in line," said the long-time client. Such are the relationships that are built in a customer-focused selling process.

Principle #2. Customers do not buy light bulbs; they buy illumination.

"Solution selling" is the buzz-phrase of modern sales. But for many sales professionals, that's just a label. They will contact a customer to "talk about the solutions we have to offer." In that sentence, solution is really just a euphemism for product.

A solution is not prepackaged. To sell a solution, you must understand the problem. But you shouldn't assume that because a customer is shopping for a light bulb, his problem is darkness. It's a simplistic example, but to sell light bulbs successfully, you need to understand why the customer wants illumination. If the customer intends to read a book, perhaps a sixty-watt bulb is called for. But if the customer intends to watch movies, decorate a Christmas tree, protect the grounds of his home, or offer someone a romantic dinner, he has a very different need. He might need an arc lamp or he might need a candle. He relies on you, the sales professional, to be the illumination expert.

Principle #3. Ignorance is a temporary condition, not a moral failing.

Many sales professionals never uncover enough information about their customers. One of the reasons is that they feel they should be experts and are afraid to betray any sign of ignorance. But ignorance is a gift to the sales professional. It's an excuse to ask a question. The question, "Could you explain that to me?" is a powerful selling tool. Most customers are delighted to explain aspects of their business to anyone who is truly interested. And any explanation a customer offers tells you more about her needs.

Customers are offended by ignorance when the sales professional tries to hide it. Hiding ignorance is the practice of the poser. Sincere ignorance (and the desire to overcome it) is the mark of an engaged sales professional.

Principle #4. Selling begins long before the sales call.

That we see value in ignorance is no excuse to avoid doing research. Prospecting itself is a matter of research: finding the companies that may need your product and then finding the people in those companies empowered to buy it. But you have the best chance of advancing the sale if you approach the prospect with a good understanding of her industry and her business, because this information will show you the issues she is likely to be facing.

You walk a fine line here, because you want to have enough background to be effective but not so much that you prejudge the prospect's needs. Prejudging needs can cause you to discard information and overlook opportunities because they don't fit your mental models.

Look at it this way. Research scientists don't experiment blindly. They form hypotheses in order to give their research some direction. But when a hypothesis becomes a hindrance rather than an aid to understanding, the responsible scientist discards it. You have to approach customers with the same agnostic attitude: form a rough picture of the customer's need, but be ready to refine it as you gather more information.

Research is not difficult in the modern world. If your company has a customer relationship management (CRM) system, it probably has a fairly complete record of any customer's history with your products or services. If you have access to the Internet, you can easily obtain company annual reports, 10-K statements (the 10-K report is a particular kind of annual report, standardized for investors), product reviews, profiles, and other documents. At the very least, don't call on a prospect without first Googling him (and remember, he has probably already Googled you).

Principle #5. The better the salesperson understands the customer's perspective, the more likely the sale will be made.

Under the Socratic Selling discipline, sales is fundamentally a cooperative process. That means the salesperson and the customer work together to meet the customer's needs. It probably goes without saying that adopting the customer's perspective gives you a better chance of understanding his needs.

The sale occurs when you link the customer's needs to the product or service you are selling. You know the ins and outs of the product or service. The customer knows the needs. When you understand the needs, you can become the link between them.

Principle #6. Customers have needs they don't always see.

Most sales models are based on limiting the sales call conversation to the immediate need and the product that might meet it. Many models even encourage listening as a way of putting customers at ease. But Socratic Selling, because it is based on understanding the customer's perspective, encourages the customer to think out loud or develop visions of the future.

Customers can discover things about their situations when they think out loud. And discoveries can mean sales opportunities. Visions of the future imply future needs.

Socratic questioning helps to bring the customer to an understanding of all needs, even those she isn't consciously aware of.

Principle #7. In the sales process, the successful salesperson spends more time listening than doing anything else.

When you're talking, you're not listening. When you're not listening, you're not gathering information, which means you're getting no closer to linking your product or service to the customer's need. And when you're not listening, you're not building the relationship.

We suggest that at least half your time in a sales call should be devoted to listening. The time for talking is when you present your proposal, which you should not do until you've gathered enough information. Until then, your talk should consist exclusively of questions designed to encourage the customer to talk.

The exception is when the customer asks you a question. When the customer asks a question, you should answer it as briefly as you can, then follow up with another question: "I'm curious. Why do you ask?"

Principle #8. Listening is an active, not passive, behavior.

The techniques of active listening were first developed by the psychologist Carl Rogers. He discovered that one of these techniques, reflecting, put clients at ease by letting them know the therapist cared enough to listen to what they were saying.

We don't need to understand the particulars of Rogers' psychological theories to take advantage of his discovery that people like it when someone listens to them. It is one of those strange ironies that Rogers called his brand of therapy "client-centered therapy." If ever there were an activity that ought to be client-centered, it's therapy! But Rogers' choice of that name implied that previous therapies were therapist-centered.

Socratic Selling aims to perform a similar function for sales: to make it customer-centered. The Socratic sales professional uses a few simple techniques of active listening to stay alert and focused on the customer's story.

Principle #9. The customer makes the decision that continues the sales process; the customer makes the decision that completes the sale.

Socratic Selling is based on the understanding that the customer is in control of the sales call. Every moment you remain in the customer's presence is the result of the customer's decision to have you there. When the customer sees no value in continuing the meeting, it will end. And the sale will not close until the customer recognizes that your proposal offers the best way to meet his need.

This is why we think the trial close is so fruitlessly manipulative. If it's time to ask the customer for the sale, ask for the sale. Don't try to find a way to ask for it without really asking for it. There's no disrespect in a direct question if you pose it at the right time.

In later chapters, we will explain in more detail how to apply the nine principles to sales work, but we suspect at this point you've had enough theory to last you for a while. In the next chapter we are going to share practical advice you can use in the first meeting with your customer.

Chapter
3

OPENING THE
FIRST MEETING

There are two kinds of customers—consumers and business customers. Typically, business customers require more sales meetings than consumers. Much of consumer selling is done in a single meeting. The categories are not hard and fast, of course. When a consumer purchases a capital good, such as an automobile or a house, the process often requires many sales meetings.

As a general rule, however, business sales involve more money, require more meetings, and demand more strategy than consumer sales. That is why we will focus on business sales. The principles are the same, but the consumer salesperson may not always get the opportunity to apply them.

The first meeting in the sales process is critical. And in business sales, the salesperson's principal goal in this meeting may simply be to arrange for the next meeting.

There is a great deal of planning that goes on before the sales call, including research, strategy, and goal-setting. You should do this planning no matter what kind of approach you take to the selling process. We've put our description of it near the end of the book, in chapter fifteen. That's because we wanted to focus your attention on the questioning and listening (which are the essential skills of Socratic Selling).

Don't Start with the Product

In chapter one, we criticized the Dooley character for trying to open the sales meeting by shouting, "It gets thirty miles to the gallon." What's wrong with opening the meeting by announcing an important feature of your product? For one thing, product features are irrelevant to customers.

Here are a few product features that most customers don't care about:

- contains fluoride
- available in six different colors
- 512 megabytes of RAM
- solid state construction
- dual overhead camshafts

It may seem heretical for us to say that customers don't care about such things, but the truth is, product features mean very little to customers. Customers are interested in benefits. Fluoride is only important because it reduces tooth decay. Lots of RAM is only important because it allows you work faster and free up your time for other activities. Availability in six colors is only important if one of the six is a color you want (and even then, it may only be important because it makes you more visible for safety's sake, keeps you stylish, or attracts members of the opposite sex). The customer is not interested in features. The customer is only interested in the benefits those features offer.

Finding the Benefit

If your product stands to benefit the customer, you have a powerful sales proposition. But there is no sales proposition evident in "It gets thirty miles to the gallon." It is a description of a feature, not a benefit.

That doesn't mean, however, that the Dooley character should have opened his meeting in chapter one by shouting, "It saves you money on gasoline." Besides being entirely too aggressive for most customers, an assertion like that isn't meaningful to everybody. Even if regular unleaded gasoline is selling for more than three dollars per gallon, saving gas money isn't an unqualified benefit for everybody. Good mileage can mean fewer trips to the gas station; it can give you good feelings about energy conservation; and it can be your personal stick in the eye of the oil companies.

Trying to imagine all the benefits of a particular feature is one way to discover your sales proposition, but it's not a very good one. You can't just draw up a list of benefits and fire them at a customer until one sticks.

What you must do is learn what the customer's needs and problems are. Then the benefits will take care of themselves.

The Fantasy of Control

In discussing the opener, most books on selling offer instruction on how to "take command" or "get control" of the sales meeting. The principle of taking control of the sales meeting is part of the agenda-focused behavior we criticized in chapter one. The idea is that the meeting will follow an agenda set by the salesperson; it will realize the salesperson's goals.

The notion of taking control of the sales meeting is nothing more than fantasy. As long as the customer is the only one capable of producing the outcome the salesperson wants (by signing the order form), the customer is in control. Believing that you can establish control of the meeting is worse than a waste of time and energy. It can lead you to act like you are in control, and as long as you're acting that way, you're unlikely to be doing your real job, which is to learn about the customer's needs.

If you must have an agenda for your first meeting with a customer, let it consist of two items:

1. Begin establishing a relationship with the customer

2. Find out the customer's needs

These two items work together. The better you understand the customer's needs, the stronger a relationship you establish with him. The stronger your relationship, the more likely he is to open up about his needs.

After the small talk and the little jokes that help take the edge off, you will sense it is time to get down to business. That's a critical moment. And even if you don't shout, "It gets thirty miles to the gallon," there are still a number of other ways you could handle it badly.

Opening Badly

When the small talk is finished, the customer will most likely expect you to begin the business part of the meeting. At this point, many sales professionals feel it's time for the presentation. They pull out the briefing book or start up PowerPoint on the laptop and launch into "Who we are and what we can do for you."

But a moment's reflection will tell you that this is a waste of both your time and the customer's. If the customer already knows who you are and what you can do for her—say, through a referral or through your company's excellent marketing—then you're just going over the same old stuff. And if she doesn't know who you are, she doesn't care. What she cares about are those needs that are bothering her and, frankly, she wishes somebody would ask her about them—in a nice way, of course.

Starting with a presentation or even with a brief description of your company won't move the sales process along at all. In fact, following Socratic Selling principles, you should not make a presentation during the first meeting with a customer. The time to make the presentation is after you've learned the nature of the customer's needs. Then you can make a presentation on how you're going to meet them. Keep the canned presentation in your briefcase.

Some sales trainers advise you to open with a question, and that's better than opening with a presentation, but it's only effective if it's the right question. And the right question is not, as we've heard some sales trainers advise, "How do you feel about our product?" Yes, it's important to get access to the customer's worldview, but how much opinion is the average customer likely to have about a product she hasn't bought yet?

Bad openers are usually the result of the salesperson trying to gain control of the meeting. What you need to do to open the meeting, however, is turn over control to the customer. It's the only way you're going to find out what the customer's needs are.

The Socratic Opener

The essence of Socratic selling is asking questions. The purpose of an opener, then, is to get the customer talking so you can begin questioning. The opener must 1) address the business issue at hand, 2) encourage the customer to talk about her needs, and 3) begin to build a relationship between you and the customer by establishing a cooperative goal.

The Socratic opener is a three-part formula. Here's an example in which the parts are separated by commas:

I'm prepared to discuss _____, but if you could give me your thoughts on it first, we can focus on what's important to you.

The blank, of course, signifies whatever you promised to base the meeting on: "what we talked about on the phone," "the new communications technology," or even (if you already understand the customer's needs) "your problem with increased defects."

This one short sentence may seem informal, but its three clauses are a precise formula that will launch the sales process.

1. Announce your preparation. "I'm prepared to discuss _____" lets the customer know that you're focused on the business at hand. That's the minimum you need to do in this part of the opener. In fact, this is also a good place to advertise some of the work you've done to reach this state of preparation:

- "I've been looking at your company website, and I'm prepared to discuss_____"

- "I have been studying the problems of this industry, and I'm prepared to discuss_____"

- "I've read your last three annual reports, and I'm prepared to discuss_____"

When you describe your preparation, you signal to the customer how important she is. Everyone likes being reminded of how important they are. The trick is to do it subtly enough that it doesn't seem like ordinary flattery. Giving a brief account of the effort you've put into understanding the customer's position in the industry is a sincere and subtle way to do it.

2. Invite the customer to share his perspective. The second part, "but if you could give me your thoughts on it first," is the part of the opener that does the heavy lifting. This is a request for the customer to talk. It is stated simply in this example, but a moment's reflection will tell you there are lots of ways to say this:

- "if you could tell me where you stand"

- "if you could bring me up to date on your thinking"

- "if you could help me understand what you want to accomplish"

3. Offer a benefit for answering. The third part of the opener, "we can focus on what's important to you," is your promise to the customer that answering your question will save time and keep the meeting on track. Some other formulations:

- "we can make the best use of your time"

- "we can make sure we cover your agenda"

or even simply

- "we'll talk about that first"

The middle part of the formula is the important part. The other parts are there to smooth the way into it and to make answering attractive to the customer.

Most customers are perfectly happy to talk about their perspective on the matter at hand, and getting them to do so is your best chance of starting a dialogue that will ultimately get you to their needs. And their needs, of course, are your key to the successful sale.

Chapter
4

WHY
SOCRATIC SELLING
WORKS

Now that we've seen what Socratic Selling isn't and we've had a taste of its technique, let's talk a little about how it does what it does.

Although Socrates repeatedly insisted he was too ignorant for the role, he was nevertheless a teacher. And his method of teaching was to ask questions. Answering the questions helped his students learn about life by both clarifying their understanding and building on it. Just because it didn't work so well with the more complacent classes of Athenian society doesn't mean the method was flawed. It just doesn't work with people who think they have no need for the truth. For those who do have the need, the method succeeds brilliantly.

One of the reasons it succeeds so well is that it is based on the notion that students are smart enough to figure things out, which is to say it respects them. People respond readily to that kind of respect.

Socratic Selling works the same way. It is based on respect for the customer. It is a discipline for helping them clarify their needs. We use the word "discipline" with some care, for that is the way it must be practiced to be successful. The Socratic salesperson must discipline herself to listen and to probe.

Sales Professionals Like to Talk

In over a decade of teaching this method to sales professionals, we have repeatedly surveyed our students on what they see as their deficiencies. And every time we do the survey, the largest proportion of them—by a wide margin—report that they talk too much. (Not coincidentally, this is the same deficiency in sales professionals most widely reported by customers.)

It's understandable. Sales professionals like to talk. It's one of the reasons that many of them go into sales— the chance to talk to and maintain relationships with a wide variety of people. But to succeed in Socratic Selling, you have to discipline yourself to give up talking.

What you must remember is that it's not your job to invent needs for the customer. The needs are already there. The best you can do is to help the customer recognize and clarify the existing needs.

The Socratic salesperson uses four basic skills:
- preparing
- listening
- questioning
- working through issues

The activities tend to occur in the order they are presented here, but it's important to remember they are not steps. The customer, in fact, should not be aware of the process. He should just experience conversation that leads him to recognize the need to buy from you.

Preparing. We will save our discussion of preparation until the end of the book in order to make listening and questioning the primary focus. Preparation is important, but it is much the same no matter what kind of approach you take to the sales process. Before you even meet the prospect, you need to know a great deal about the prospect himself, the nature of the prospect's business, and the nature of the prospect's industry. With this background information in hand, you plan what you are to achieve—first in the overall sales cycle, and then in the individual sales call.

In the age of the world wide web and the customer relationship management (CRM) system, there is no excuse for approaching a sales call without a good understanding of the customer's business, competitive position, advantages and threats, markets, recent history, and history with your company. It's a great deal easier to recognize significant information that comes to you during a call if you have a notion of what you're looking for, which is why we used the comparison earlier to a research scientist beginning her inquiry with a hypothesis. You use the information gleaned during your research to formulate an idea of a customer's needs, then refine or change that idea as you listen to the customer.

Listening. Listening is a skill the Socratic salesperson uses throughout the sales process, even the preparation phase, which may involve interviewing people.

Having prepared and developed a strategy, you call on the customer and, using the Socratic Opener described in the previous chapter, begin to get the customer's story. You listen actively to the customer's story and confirm your understanding of it. Your listening skills actually encourage the customer to talk, which provides more opportunity for listening, which encourages the customer to talk, and so forth. This can become a self-sustaining process.

One of the reasons Socratic salespeople are so successful is that they gain so much information. The more information you have about your customer, the better chance you will have of showing him the connection between his needs and what you are selling.

Questioning. The Socratic salesperson moves seamlessly from listening to questioning. In fact, some types of questioning—particularly the query "tell me more"—are an integral part of active listening.

The questioning is not random. You are guided in your questioning by the strategy you create during your preparation and by what you've learned so far of the customer's story.

You ask questions that will help you understand, or refine your understanding of, the customer's current state, the state that led to it, and what stands between the customer and his goals. This information helps you to form a picture of the customer's motivators, both in business and personal terms.

Once you've made your proposal to the customer, you continue to use your questioning skills—to probe for the reasons behind her questions and objections, which are rarely what they initially seem to be.

Working through Issues. Your questioning and listening skills allow you to understand the customer's needs as well as the customer does, maybe better. But along the way, as you work creatively to show the customer how your product or service meets his need, there are obstacles. The customer asks hard questions or raises objections.

In dealing with these questions and objections, you need to use your questioning skills to discover what's really behind them. But when you discover the real issues, you need to have the skill to work through them. This skill consists of knowing your limits (sometimes you need to simply walk away from a deal) and coming up with creative ways to reduce obstacles ("I can give you the price you want if you give me some flexibility on delivery time.").

But the most important part of the working-through-issues skill is the creativity you must use to help the customer see how your product or service meets his need. If you can make the connection between his need and what you're selling, you make the sale. If you can't make the connection, you are unlikely to make the sale, nor should you want to. Selling something to a customer who has no need for it doesn't work over the long term. Such sales are often cancelled, and a cancelled sale is worse than no sale because it incurs much more cost.

And of course the biggest issue you work through is whether the customer will actually give you the order. Unlike most selling approaches in which the closing is like the climax in an adventure movie, in Socratic Selling, the closing is more like a foregone conclusion. Socratic salespeople often report it as anticlimactic.

If you plotted the sale by the amount of time spent using each skill, it should come out so that Preparing and Working through Issues each take up about one eighth of the process. Questioning takes up one quarter. Listening takes up half.

These are just rough guidelines, but the point is that listening is far and away the most important activity in the process. It is your chief research and relationship-building tool, and it should be your principal method for relating to the customer.

Chapter
5

GETTING THE
CUSTOMER'S STORY

You have made your Socratic Opener. At this point, you have probably used three to five minutes breaking the ice with small talk and turning down the customer's offer of coffee. You did turn it down, didn't you?

OK. Let's make a brief detour here. Don't drink the customer's coffee. Caffeine elevates your heart rate, increases your blood pressure, and reduces your ability to keep still. These are not the processes you want to have acting on your body during the stress of a sales call. And if you think you can just opt for decaffeinated coffee, remember that coffee is a major contributor to bad breath, and it's one of the most difficult odors to mask with breath mints. Drink your coffee early, before you go to work, and give yourself enough time to cleanse your breath. If the customer offers you something to drink and you don't want to turn it down, take water.

OK. Let's get back to our regularly scheduled text.

You and the customer have no doubt already agreed on how long this meeting will last. So far, you have used three to five minutes for small talk and turning down coffee and thirty to forty-five seconds for the Socratic Opener. In whatever time remains, you must begin the process of getting the customer's story.

The Customer Responds to the Opener

You have invited the customer to provide his perspective on the matter you're discussing. Customers are human beings, and human beings aren't always predictable. You could hear almost anything in response to the opener, which is why we cannot script this. We can only tell you what to listen for.

The first thing to listen for is history. Most customers will start with that, if for no other reason than it's a subject in which they are experts. The historical account may go something like, "For the past year, we've been doing about 10,000 copies a month…"

History is important, and if you sell copiers, the 10,000-per-month figure is probably significant to you. Take note of it as a useful piece of information. But the most important part is what the customer will probably say next. And the next thing the customer says is likely to be engaging, wary, insulting, or irrelevant.

Engagement

Sometimes a customer is actually already considering you as a possible source of help with a problem. In that case, whatever she says after the history may be followed by something that actually addresses what you're here for:

> *"For the past year, we've been doing about 10,000 copies a month, and I'm concerned about the cost of consumables."*

Be careful of the engaged customer, because her enthusiasm will tempt you to rush the process. Many sales professionals will come right back at the customer: "If you're concerned about the cost of consumables, then you'll be interested to know the Supreme copier has the lowest consumables cost of all major copiers." This is a mistake.

For one thing, an aggressive assertion like that can scare the customer away. For another thing, trying to get to the close too quickly prevents you from gathering more information. At this stage, you want to gather information, because you need to make sure that the cost of consumables is the real issue. And even if it turns out to be the real issue, gathering more information may open more sales opportunities.

So, even though things look very promising at this point, curb your enthusiasm and probe for more of the story.

Wariness

The customer who begins with a story that broaches a clear need, however, is probably the exception. It's more likely you'll have a wary customer who will follow the history with something highly ambiguous:

> *"For the past year, we've been doing 10,000 copies a month on our Acme copiers, but I thought I should look and see what else is available."*

In this case, the customer doesn't want to reveal a need. Your goal is simply to get more information about the customer's situation, and if he is wary, to make him comfortable. One way to do that is to take the conversation in the direction of his expertise. As we noted above, the customer always has expertise in the history, so that's often a safe place to follow up, particularly if you've been listening closely.

Insult

Sometimes you'll get a response that a sensitive person would consider a slap in the face:

> *"For the past year, we've been doing 10,000 copies a month, and I've been delighted with the performance of our Acme copiers.*
> *We love Acme."*

If you're there to sell Supreme copiers, you will be tempted to take offense. Don't. People do a lot of strange things when they're scared.

Did we say scared?

It's a little-appreciated quality of customers that they are fearful. What are they afraid of? They are afraid of being sold! Very few customers understand that you are here to solve their problems. They think you are here to sell them, by which they mean to take money from them. And as long as the customer fears you, he's not going to buy.

The insulting customer presents you with two requirements: You must not only probe, but also make her fear go away. Make sure you look the customer in the eye and offer a warm smile. Above all, whatever the customer says in response to the opener, treat it seriously.

Many sales professionals, on being told the customer loves a competitor's product, will be dismissive. But if you dismiss anything the customer says, you are dismissing the customer—not a good way to treat somebody who could spend a lot of money with you.

If being dismissive is bad, badmouthing the competitor's product is even worse. There's obvious badmouthing: "Some of my accounts have told me they have a lot of trouble with those." And there's more subtle badmouthing: "I imagine you have developed a lot of expertise in dealing with the servicing issues." But badmouthing a competitor's product, even if you're subtle about it, makes you look insecure.

Other sales professionals may keep from bad-mouthing the competitor's product but will try to change the subject: "Have you ever considered trying another brand?" This is marginally better than bad-mouthing the other product, but it's another form of dismissiveness. The customer owns this conversation, and changing the subject amounts to trying to take it away from him.

Irrelevance

The Socratic Opener is one of the best tools ever invented for beginning the process of getting the customer's story. But customers are human beings, and they don't always react the way you might expect them to. Sometimes you will get a response that is simply irrelevant:

> *"For the past year, we've been doing 10,000 copies a month.*
>
> *Do you have kids? How do you handle it when they steal a car and spend the night in jail?"*

When the customer responds with irrelevance, you may have to resign yourself to a conversation that has nothing to do with your purpose in being there. As we said, changing the subject amounts to wresting control of the conversation from the customer, which is futile and potentially offensive.

Particularly when you get a customer (admittedly rare) who wants to talk about personal problems, you have no choice but to listen. When a customer chooses to share this part of his life with you, there's both good news and bad news. The good news is that your Socratic efforts are working. He trusts you, and you're on your way to creating a relationship that has meaning for him beyond his professional responsibilities. The bad news is that he's not ready to talk about buying anything, and whatever you do to get the conversation back to that is likely to disrupt the trust, perhaps by betraying insensitivity, perhaps by embarrassing him. The rest of the sales call will probably be devoted to your listening to stories about the customer's teenaged son. Forget about doing any business; just concentrate on building the relationship until the customer can recover his professional frame of mind.

The Nature of Questions

You always respond to the customer's response with another question. As anyone who has ever taken an SAT exam knows, there are two kinds of questions: open and closed. Closed questions are those you answer by choosing a brief response from those offered:

> *"Which pair of socks do you prefer, the red or the green?"*

In this case, the questioner offers the choice between red and green. Questions you answer with "yes" or "no" are also closed questions.

In Socratic Selling, you don't usually offer the customer choices, because when you offer choices, you don't learn very much. Asking, "Do you like your Acme copiers?" is not an effective probe because the answer (either "yes" or "no") cuts off, or at least reduces the need for, further conversation.

Open questions, on the other hand, offer no choices, so they tend to generate new information. "What do you like about your Acme copiers?" will cause the customer to discuss her needs or her problem. She might cite their speed, their reliability, their economy, their ease of service. You have opened a new line of inquiry and suddenly you're learning a great deal about the customer's requirements.

Open questions usually begin with these words:

- "What…"
- "Why…"
- "How…"
- "Give me an example…"

Whatever the customer says after the opener should help you formulate your first open question.

Probe for Facts, Probe for Emotions

Later in the sales process, you will use questions—Socratic probes—to correct or modify your understanding, to confirm your understanding, or to improve the specificity of your understanding. We'll cover how to do all those things later in the book. At this point, however, you will probably want to use probes mainly to gather more information.

Responding to the Engaged Customer

Try to base your probe on the last thing the customer said, because that's likely to be the important part, and it's the direction in which she wants to go. With the engaged customer, this is easy. To her "I'm concerned about the cost of consumables," you can come back with an open question, "Why are you concerned?" If that seems too bald a way to put it, say, "Tell me more about your concerns."

Any time the customer specifies a concern or interest, it's an invitation to you to follow up on it, and the "tell me more" response is quite effective for that.

Why shouldn't you simply treat the customer's concern as a statement that she considers the consumables too expensive? Because she may not. It could be the case that it's not the cost of consumables that concerns her as much as handling or storing them. Or she may be concerned about the cost of employee downtime in replenishing them. Or she may simply be concerned about how much toner she has spilled on her clothes because of the current copiers' awkward replenishment system. Even if the case is no more or less than what she first stated, you'll benefit from more information about it.

Responding to the Wary Customer

If you have a wary customer, of course, he hasn't provided much in the second part of his response to follow up on. If there's nothing in the second part to follow up on, follow up on the first part:

"You said you've been doing 10,000 copies a month for the past year, but it sounds like it's a new situation. What happened a year ago?"

Your goal here is to draw the customer out. Keep the dialogue going and keep the customer talking, because talking will increase his comfort level.

Responding to the Insulting Customer

The customer who tells you she likes a competitor's product is probably a little afraid. Treat her the same way you treat the wary customer: draw her out.

"You said you love your Acme copiers. What is it you love about them?"

You're likely to get some interesting and usable information here. You will certainly learn something about the customer's needs.

Responding to Irrelevance

It is especially important to base your probe on what the customer has said when the customer's response expresses some emotion. We all strive to drain the emotion from business interactions, so there is a tendency among sales professionals, when they hear emotions in a customer assertion, to avoid them and shift back to the passionless discussion of business. But if a customer actually favors you with personal emotions, like the one in the example of irrelevancy cited above, it's an opportunity to build the relationship. The best way to do that is to probe the emotion. You probe emotions by reflecting them:

> *"It sounds like your son's behavior is causing you some anxiety."*

You may feel a little like a therapist, and in fact reflecting emotion is a technique from Rogerian counseling. But reflecting is a way to notice emotion in a customer's conversation. And everybody is entitled to notice emotions, whether they've had training in therapy or not.

We'll discuss reflecting emotion more when we get to the section on active listening.

The point is, when there's an emotional component to the customer's conversation, it's important to follow up on it. This follow-up may get you no closer to understanding the customer's needs, but it will build the relationship.

Somewhere in the customer's response to your opener is the key to your next move. Listen carefully to the response and use whatever you find in it—facts or emotions—to probe for more by means of open-ended questions or reflecting emotion.

Chapter
6

THEORIES OF CUSTOMER MOTIVATION

A s you continue to probe your customer Socratically, you will form a picture of the customer's needs. Matching your product to her needs, of course, is a major step in making the sale. Customers don't ordinarily buy things that don't meet a need or solve a problem.

While matching your product to the customer's need is a necessary step to making a sale, however, it's not enough. In addition to the need, the customer has emotions about the need, and the sale will depend on whether you effectively address those emotions. It's time to look at motivation.

Background on Motivation

Scientists agree that there are three types of motivation:
- biological
- learned
- cognitive

Biological motivations are in some ways easiest to understand. They consist of basic drives like hunger, thirst, and sex. They are straightforward, although the infinitely variable ways in which people satisfy them often aren't.

Learned motivations are less straightforward and result from conditioning. Pavlov's dogs learned the motivation that made them salivate at the ringing of a bell. In another primitive experiment, a child was conditioned to associate a noise he feared with the appearance of a white rat. Eventually, the white rat alone could provoke the child's fear. The fear felt at the rat's appearance was a learned motivation. Many phobias are learned motivations. Most significant for our purposes, however, is that the desire for money is largely a learned motivation. Few people want money for what it is; they want it for what they associate it with. They associate it with comfort, security, abundance, and so forth. Nearly all of us have been conditioned to be motivated by money. This is one of the reasons that so many advertisers base their marketing messages on price. The desire for money is one of the few learned motivations that is almost universal. Other learned motivations may be much more difficult to recognize or even understand.

Cognitive motivations arise from people's reasoning and are typically associated with goals. They are based on expectations. They drive us to behave in ways that we think will make us successful. Social behaviors and work behaviors are generally driven by cognitive motivations. We act on cognitive motivations not because of immediate desires, but because of our capacity to predict that achieving certain goals will ultimately fulfill our desires. The difference between a learned motivation and a cognitive motivation is the difference between ordering a pizza and building one yourself from scratch.

In the corporate context, the desire to get and keep money is a cognitive motivation as well as a learned one. Corporations must attend to the bottom line, and they impart a drive to save or earn money to nearly all their employees. Even if you somehow managed to grow up in modern society without a learned motivation to get and keep money, when you go to work for a corporation, the corporation will put it into your job description. Nearly every employee has a cognitive motivation around money. The motivation may not always be to acquire money, but we all at least have a motivation not to lose it.

Just because cognitive motivations are the result of reasoning doesn't mean they are devoid of emotion. Going to college so you can have a well-paying job after graduation is a cognitive motivation, but for most people it's an emotionally charged decision.

Helping the Customer Form a Motivation

Of course, our primary concern should be cognitive motivations, since the purchase of a complex product will involve the customer's goals, as opposed to his gratification.

Biological motivations are roughly similar in all human beings. People are individual in their level of control of these motivators, but that doesn't really concern us, because we are rarely in the position to make use of those motivations anyway. Yes, if you invite a customer to breakfast (not a bad idea!), you can watch the customer's hunger motivation in action. But satisfying his hunger would be only incidental to the sales process. Nobody is going to trade a major purchase decision for a breakfast.

We can safely ignore biological motivations and concentrate on learned and cognitive motivations. In other words, we want to help the customer form the cognitive motivation to buy while recognizing that there may be learned motivations that will come into play.

Just because there is an emotional component in a motivation doesn't mean it's irrational. The customer's purchase decision should always rest on business reasons. The purchase must meet some business need. But within that need, the customer has personal needs. The right purchase may help her keep her job or get promoted. It may increase the influence of her department. This is another way of saying the customer has both business and personal goals. The sale may not occur until both are satisfied.

Varieties of Cognitive Motivation

What drives, then, can we recognize as cognitive motivations? Common sense says that people are driven by a desire for money. But modern research on motivation has shown that money is only one drive among many, and it may not be the most important one.

A great deal of modern motivational theory has been pressed into service on behalf of business managers, who need to know how to direct the behavior of subordinates. There are at least half a dozen theories of work motivation that have been proposed by psychologists and supported by research and experiment. You can find good summaries of them in any decent textbook on organizational behavior.

Three Predominant Needs

Fortunately, we don't need to review all the theories since most of them—addressing concepts like job design and employee morale—are irrelevant. There is one theory, however, that helps explain buying behavior. Through the 1960s and 1970s, psychologist David McClelland and his associates developed a model of cognitive motivation based on three needs:

- achievement
- power
- affiliation

McClelland found that people with a high need for achievement seek situations in which they get personal responsibility for a project's success or failure, immediate feedback on performance, and moderate challenges. People with a high need for power tend to be competitive and seek situations that give them influence and prestige, which they value more than they value effective performance. People with a high need for affiliation seek situations of cooperative effort and mutual understanding.

This is not to say that the whole world consists of three kinds of people. All people probably share these three drives to some extent, but each of us has an individual mix of them. And who's to say there aren't more drives that McClelland never found? The purpose of this description of motivational theory is to help you recognize and appreciate motivations that are different from your own. Of all the dimensions of human individuality, the difference in motivations is probably the one that causes the most misunderstanding. If you have a high need for achievement, that doesn't mean all your customers do. You need to learn to recognize the drives for power and affiliation so you can help customers realize them.

It's important to remember, too, that motivation is not a button you push to elicit a certain kind of behavior. Motivation is more like an insight into how a person views the world, because recognizing it helps you understand his goals.

Applying the Motivational Model

What are some of the practical uses of McClelland's needs-based model? Research has shown that successful managers tend to have a high need for power. If your customer is a successful manager, you may hypothesize that she is motivated by power.

On the other hand, the movers and shakers of an organization tend to have high achievement needs. If your customer is an entrepreneur, you could hypothesize that he has a high achievement need.

People with a high affiliation need tend to be team players. They're often found in larger organizations because it is easy to be uncomfortable in a small organization when you have a strong need for affiliation.

When you see signs of one of these needs in a customer, use open questions to bring it to the surface:

- "How will this affect the performance of your division?" (Achievement)
- "How will this affect your division's standing in the company?" (Power)
- "How will this affect the morale in the division?" (Affiliation)

The enthusiasm with which a customer answers such questions may help you to understand her predominant driver.

Understanding your customer's motivation will help you to understand her goals. When you can explain how the benefits of your product will help the customer reach her goals, both business and personal, you are that much closer to the sale.

Chapter
7

PROBING THE CUSTOMER'S STORY

At this point, you've gotten a glimpse of the customer's story. You need to continue to question and to listen in order to form a better understanding.

To give your listening some structure, look for the type of needs your customer is feeling while you probe. Needs tend to come in three types:

- problem (an obstacle that stands between your customer and the achievement of a goal)
- opportunity (a chance for an advantage in achieving a goal)
- weakness (a deficiency that undermines your customer's effectiveness in striving toward a goal).

It's easiest to understand a problem-type need, because that's the kind a customer will talk about most readily:

- *"Frankly, I'm concerned about the cost of consumables."*

- *"Deliveries are taking too long."*
- *"Our older employees don't understand the importance of service."*

Opportunity-type needs are much more subtle. In fact, the customer may not even be aware of them. They relate to a customer's competitive position or ability to exploit undeveloped markets.

And customers will not often reveal a weakness unless you have a long-standing relationship and a great deal of trust.

Remember that your goal is not to identify for the customer the type of needs you discover. Save that for your proposal. Your goal at this point is to understand them. The way you do that is get the customer to talk and keep talking.

Expand and Specify

As the customer begins to relate the story, there are two basic directions in which to probe: expansion and specificity. With expanding probes, you are asking the customer to broaden the information she is giving you. Use prompts such as:

- *"Tell me more."*
- *"Why do you say that?"*
- *"Please elaborate on…"*

With specifying probes, you ask the customer to narrow down information:

- *"Give me an example."*
- *"How does that work?"*
- *"Why do you say that?"*

To give some direction to your probing, look for motivation, both business and personal.

Probing for Business Motivations

Obviously, profit is the lowest common denominator among business motivations and the end result that customers strive for. But there are a lot of ways to get to a profit, and any one of them can be a business motivation:

- higher sales
- lower costs
- higher productivity
- more efficient production
- reduced staff turnover
- increased employee morale
- reduced risk
- increased market share

There are many others, and your ability to find them may be limited only by the limits of your attentiveness.

As you get the customer to talk about the needs of the business, listen for clues about his motivations and probe with open-ended questions. Ask

- What's at risk for the company?

- What else is at risk?
- How does this affect market opportunities?
- What impact will this have
    - on sales?
    - on staff turnover?
    - on productivity?
    - on costs?

Take your cue from what the customer says (and what your research has turned up) about the company's mission, goals, problems, and opportunities.

Probing for Personal Motivations

Customers have their own concerns as well. They have goals just like you do, and if you can find a way to help them reach their personal goals while meeting the business need, you increase the likelihood of making the sale.

Customers' personal goals have to do with status, job security, achievement, opportunity, and other drivers you need to discover. This doesn't mean personal goals are necessarily selfish. A customer's personal goals often align with the goals of the company, at least as the customer perceives them. Listen for clues and probe with open-ended questions:

- How does this affect your company?
- Why is this important to you?
- How does this affect your team's ability to succeed?
- What impact will this have on departmental goals?

Your open-ended probes will begin to bring more of the customer's story to the surface. As the customer speaks, you need to listen.

How Not to Listen

Most people have two states in a conversation: speaking and waiting to speak. Waiting to speak is a bad listening habit. If you're waiting to speak, it means you're thinking about what you want to say, which means you're not listening.

What are some other common bad listening habits? Focusing on the speaker rather than the speech is one. If you're paying attention to the customer's clothing, physical appearance, accent, or accessories, you're probably not paying attention to what is being said. You need to practice taking in those kinds of details before you even get to the opener.

Another bad listening habit is ignoring what you don't understand. We all do this, partly because we're hesitant to interrupt the speaker and partly because we fear being seen as ignorant. But when you find something in the customer's conversation you don't understand, it's a gift, because it's an opportunity to ask for clarification, which means more and better information about the customer's needs. Whenever the customer says something you don't understand, wait until she finishes her thought, then ask her what she meant.

We often let our emotions interfere with listening, too. If the customer says something that presses one of your buttons, there's a natural human tendency to tune him out and focus on your emotions. Perhaps you're a conservative, for example, and your customer is a liberal. But your customer may be a liberal with a need for your product. That's not to say that you should abandon your principles just because you're a salesperson. But you should control your emotions and recognize that focusing on them has a cost, and in the immediate context of a sales call, that cost may be lost information.

The worst of the bad listening habits is interrupting. It goes without saying that when you're speaking, you're not listening. When you're not listening, you're not acquiring information about the customer. And if you actually cut the customer off to speak (even if it's to say, "No, that's not what I meant"), you lose both information and customer good will. Wait until the customer finishes before making your contribution, no matter how urgent you feel the matter is.

One of our favorite stories about interrupting is quite dramatic. The customer began telling a story about her company. The salesperson, wishing to show how focused he was on the customer, interrupted her and said, "I know. I read it in the paper." Then he went on to recount the details of what he'd read.

The customer fixed him with a flinty stare and said, "You don't know." She then lit into him.

Even when you already know what the customer has to say, let the customer talk. You're bound to learn from the conversation.

Active Listening

Normal American conversational speech is about 125 words per minute. Normal comprehension, on the other hand, can occur at 400 to 500 words per minute. In other words, you are capable of listening at a rate three to four times faster than your customer is capable of speaking. This is nothing to celebrate. It's the reason for the most common bad listening habit—daydreaming.

When you listen to someone speaking at a speed that's only about a third of your listening capability, your mind tends to fill its leftover capacity with other things. These other things can then crowd out the conversation, and you lose some of what's being said. The cure for this inevitable tendency of the mind to wander during conversation is a discipline called active listening.

Active listening is a way of giving your mind jobs to do that are concerned with the conversation. These jobs keep it focused.

First Listening Technique—Playing Back

One of the most powerful listening strategies is the technique of playing back. Listen to what the customer says and play it back.

It is particularly useful in a sales call because it helps you check your interpretation of what the customer has said. Beyond that, however, it is powerful because it forces you to process what the customer says. You can't simply repeat back the customer's own words, although you sometimes may want to do that. To keep the conversation moving, you need to deal with the meaning of what the customer says.

Playing back has the additional benefit of opening the customer up. Everyone has a desire to be understood, and playing back what the customer has said almost invariably encourages her to provide additional information.

Here's how it works:

> *Customer: When a physician asks for additional information on a treatment's side effects, she doesn't have time for the rep to page through a large manual.*
>
> *Salesperson: If I understand what you're saying, the reps need immediate access to the information.*
>
> *Customer: Yes, and they need a lot of it. Dosages, contraindications, clinical trial results, head-to-head comparisons, efficacy.*

Often, as soon as the customer sees that you understand the situation, she begins to elaborate on it.

Play back the customer's conversation as often as you can. If you feel like you're beginning to sound artificial, use a variety of lead-in phrases:

- *"Let me make sure I understand what you're saying..."*
- *"In other words, you're saying..."*
- *"I hear you saying..."*

The customer will validate your interpretation or correct it and often follow up with more information.

Second Listening Technique—Summarizing

Summarizing is like playing back, except that it happens less frequently, and it involves more than one thought.

As you process what the customer is saying, fit it together so you can summarize a list of points the customer has made. Like playing back, this has benefits at two different levels. It lets you check your understanding and it forces you to attend to what the customer is saying so you can create the summary later.

At various points in the conversation, use a lead-in phrase and then list the points the customer has made:

"Let me summarize what I've heard you say so far. You've been doing about 10,000 copies per month for the past year, ever since you started customizing the contracts for each customer. Reliability is important to you, because these copies activate the billing process. And you need a machine that can handle a wide variety of paper stocks gracefully."

Summarizing shows the customer you're listening, and that's an important part of building the relationship. But it also lets you review the progress of the conversation and set up a foundation to build the next section.

Third Listening Technique—Reflect Emotion

Reflecting is a form of playing back, but it applies to emotions rather than facts. Whenever you hear a sign of emotion in the customer's conversation, you need to acknowledge it. This shows the customer that you are attending to him as a person as well as a source of information, and it builds your relationship.

One of the best lead-in phrases for reflecting emotion is "It sounds like…"

- "It sounds like you're angry about the way that turned out."
- "It sounds like you're concerned about the way this makes your department look."
- "It sounds like you enjoyed the relationship you had with that vendor."

But there are others you can use for variety:

"I get the sense you're…"

"I hear _____ in your voice."

"And this makes you feel…"

There is another technique for reflecting emotion that is even simpler. It's called the echo. To use it, take the main word or phrase of the customer's thought and repeat it as a question:

Customer: I'm being nibbled to death by ducks.

Salesperson: Ducks?

Customer: The auditors and the regulators.

Everybody wants a piece of me.

Fourth Listening Technique—Take Notes

Our final technique of active listening is to take notes. Once again, it is an activity that forces you to concentrate on what the customer is saying. It has the additional benefit, however, of creating material you can study later.

Note-taking also builds your relationship with the customer. Taking notes on a customer's conversation immediately elevates him. It says he is important because what he is saying is important. Most customers will be flattered if you take notes.

Chapter
8

THE
OPEN QUESTION

One of our friends tells the story of dining out alone while doing a training session in Houston. She's not someone who minds being alone in restaurants. She's used to it. The only thing she doesn't like about the experience is how uncomfortable her solo dining makes the wait staff.

And this was one of those times. Our friend was content and didn't feel very much like conversation. But the waiter apparently felt sorry for her, and he took it upon himself to relieve her loneliness by engaging her in conversation.

"Are you in town on business?" he said.

"Yes," she said.

He stood there for a moment, smiling. Then, when the silence became uncomfortable, he left her with her ice water and basket of warm rolls and went to do something else.

After a few minutes, he was back again with her salad. He smiled engagingly. "Are you in oil and gas?"

"No," she said.

He stood again, smiling in the silence, then left.

It went on like that through the entire meal. He tried

- *"Are you working on a big project?"*
- *"Is this your first time visiting Houston?"*
- *"Have you been to the Space Center?"*
- *"Will you be here long?"*

She answered every question with "yes" or "no."

He was a pleasant waiter, and she had an enjoyable meal, and she even appreciated his sincerity and concern. But as a conversationalist, he was an utter failure.

He asked only closed questions. And since every question could be answered with a "yes" or a "no," she had no reason to volunteer any further information. She learned far more about him that evening than he learned about her.

She was being deliberately reticent, partly because she didn't feel like having a conversation and partly, if the truth be told, because she began to enjoy the game and wondered if the waiter would ever figure out why he couldn't get a conversation started. Your customers may not be as deliberately uncommunicative as our friend was that evening. But the point of the story is that if you want to have a conversation (indeed, if you are a salesperson and you need to have a conversation), you will not accomplish that with closed questions.

If the waiter had asked, "What brings you to Houston?" he might have gotten a little chunk of our friend's life story.

The Difficulty of Open Questions

Why is it so supremely difficult to form an open question? Why is it that, on meeting someone for the first time, we almost always start a conversation with

- *"Nice weather, isn't it?"*
- *"Do you come here often?"*
- *"Are you happy with your current supplier?"*
- *"This car's a beaut, isn't it?"*
- *"If I were able to show you right now a way you could drive away in this gorgeous red car without changing your current household budget, would we have a basis for doing business?"*

If that final question looks familiar, it should. It's the classic, high-pressure trial close. That it appears in a list of examples of closed questions is no accident. One of the purposes of a closed question is to keep the conversation in the control of the questioner.

The trial close, in addition to being an attempt to ask for the business without asking for the business, grabs control of the conversation. It is a tool of agenda-centered technique.

But Socratic Selling is not agenda-centered. It is customer-centered. The Socratic seller asks questions to get information and to build a relationship, not to control the conversation. The first step in learning to ask open questions is to force yourself to surrender control of the sales conversation. Then, don't just give the customer a choice of responses, find out what's going on inside her mind.

The Open Interrogatories

We noted in a previous chapter that open questions tend to begin with certain words:
- *"What do you think about this weather?"*
- *"Why are you here this evening?"*
- *"How do you see your business changing with a new supplier?"*
- *"Describe your ideal automobile."*
- *"Tell me more about your driving needs."*

"Describe" and "tell me more" are not strictly speaking interrogatories, but they serve the same purpose, which is to get more information. And that may be the principal difference between closed and open questions: Open questions seek information. Closed questions seek a quick answer.

The characteristics of open questions are that they tend to get long answers, they surrender control of the conversation (or confirm the other person's control), and they often receive answers that include emotions.

With a closed question, you usually know how the other person will respond (or you expect a narrow range of responses). But with an open question, there's no telling what the response will be. And for the committed Socratic seller, that's the exciting part.

The easiest way to form an open question is to use one of these five open interrogatories:
- What
- Why

- How
- Describe
- Tell me more

Even then, it can be quite difficult. Many of us discover that our imaginations are just too limited to quickly produce open questions. But that's because we are trying to imagine the answers. The way to train yourself to ask open questions is to train yourself to give up control of the conversation and hope for surprises.

When to Use Closed Questions

That's not to say that you should ask customers only open questions. There are times when closed questions are appropriate. Sometimes you want a piece of information, but you don't want an information-rich response:

- *"How many copies do you do a month?"*
- *"Who is your current supplier?"*
- *"Will you use this car for commuting?"*

Sometimes you just need some details in order to move forward.

And, of course, the classic situation for a closed question is the close. While we reject the agenda-grabbing trial close because of its dishonesty, we do recommend not pussy-footing around the close. When it's time to do business, just ask for a "yes" or "no."

But that's not for a few chapters yet.

Chapter
9

THE
DECISION MAKER

I t would be nice if you knew who was empowered to sign the order before you began the sales process, but life doesn't usually work that way. Your pre-call research (see chapter 15) may give you a hint, and you no doubt got a sense of it when you lined up the appointment to speak with the customer. But you probably won't understand the whole situation until you're in the customer's office.

You need to determine if the customer has the budget and if the customer has the power. This phase, which is usually known as "qualifying," is presented in most sales training courses and books as the first step in the sales process. That makes sense if you're selling refrigerators or automobiles, since the customer has come to you.

But if you're out there searching the landscape for customers, as we usually are in business sales, you need to delay the qualification phase until you've begun to establish the relationship. The reason is that qualification questions tend to be somewhat direct, and direct questions can frighten customers.

Fortunately, in Socratic Selling, the customer will often qualify himself when he responds to the opener. If not, then you need to formulate some questions that will help you get the lay of the land.

You will ask questions in two areas—budget and power—and our advice is not to ask them together.

Ideally, you want to ask them when they arise naturally in the conversation. Never ask a question that is unrelated to the customer's last answer. Doing so takes your conversation out of the realm of relationship-building and back into the realm of, "I'm here to sell you something." The customer knows you're here to sell her something. You don't need to remind her. Don't, for example, try to handle it like this:

> *Customer: We've used Acme copiers for several years, and we love them.*
> *Salesperson: What's your budget for new copiers?*

This is an extreme example. Few salespeople would be that clumsy. The point is, whatever the customer says to you is something he has chosen to bring into the open to show you. If you fail to follow up on it, it's the same thing as dismissing it.

Find a way to relate your qualification questions to the story the customer is telling.

Power

The customer you talk with may not always be the final decision maker. Every organization has its own way of dealing with this. The customer may not be able to finalize the order without the approval of her boss or a committee. Another may have no purchasing authority at all and may just be investigating.

Don't ask a customer if she has the authority to make the purchase. For one thing, that's a closed question and kills the opportunity for discussion about the purchase process. Secondly, a question like that can embarrass a customer who doesn't have such authority. At the very least it can make her feel like she is confessing to wasting your time.

The way to learn who holds purchasing authority is to ask about the structure of the process:

- *"Tell me about the steps involved in a purchase."*
- *"Could you describe the purchase decision criteria?"*
- *"What does the implementation calendar look like?"*

Questions like these can generate a great deal of information about the way the customer's company works. And usually, in answering, the customer will explain his role in the process. If you find out the customer doesn't have the authority to place the order, that doesn't mean you should stop selling him. It just means you have more selling to do after him and you should begin asking questions about the needs of the person who does place the order. In any case, you're likely to need the recommendation of your customer to get to the next level.

Politics

Sometimes, you may find yourself up against an intractable political situation.

One of our favorite horror stories concerns a salesperson who wanted to sell a presentation skills training program to a company. She was making good progress establishing a relationship with a company's training manager, but the training manager was fairly clear with her that the final decision rested with a committee. The salesperson knew she was up against a half dozen competitors for the job.

The salesperson, being a good Socratic seller, asked to speak with the decision makers on the committee so she could learn about their needs. The training manager asked, then came back and said the decision makers would not speak to her. Then the training manager volunteered to take some questions from the salesperson to the committee members. The salesperson submitted her questions. But when the training manager next contacted her, it was to tell her the committee refused to answer her questions. They just wanted her to come in and give her presentation before the committee.

"I knew going in that I wouldn't win this one," she said later.

When she walked into the conference room, there were six people sitting there watching her. One, whom we'll call Fred, sat with his arms folded and a grim look on his face.

"Before I start," she said, "I'd like to ask some questions about your needs."

"No questions," said Fred. "Just give your presentation."

She wasn't surprised when nobody asked her any questions afterward. And she left the conference room with a heavy heart.

Some days later, she talked with the training manager and asked her if there had been more going on in that room than people were talking about.

"Last year," said the training manager, "we brought in a training firm to teach presentation skills. Fred arranged it. The program was an utter failure." It turned out that Fred wanted to bring the same firm back in order to redeem his decision from the previous year. Everyone else in the firm was opposed to bringing the other firm back, but Fred was the most powerful person involved in the decision. Bringing in six different companies to make presentations was just part of Fred's attempt to get buy-in for a decision he'd already made.

The moral of the story is that Socratic Selling is powerful but not omnipotent. You can't use it if the customer won't share any information with you. But would you really want to do business with such a company?

In this case, the sales professional looks back on the failed sale with relief. She knows that if she'd somehow made the sale, her troubles would have only begun.

Budget

Your first concern is whether the customer has the money to buy your product. In a furniture store, the sales professional gets the information by asking, "How much do you want to spend?" It works in a furniture store, but it's inappropriate to a business sales call.

Some sales professionals will ask, "What's your budget for this?" At least that question uses the language of business. But few customers will answer such a question. They know that identifying a budget inhibits their flexibility in negotiating with you later. They know there is a minimum figure you would accept for the product or service, and they want to find the minimum before committing. They expect that if they describe a budget in excess of that minimum, you will fill the difference between the minimum and their quoted figure with add-ons—or simply pad the price to fit their budget.

But where most customers are unwilling to tell you the budget up front, they are usually willing to speculate about a hypothetical budget. So ask the customer to speculate:

> *"If you were to identify a budget for this project, what would it be?"*

If that's too direct, then ask the customer to speculate about a range:

> *"If you were to identify a budget for this project, what would the range look like?"*

It's easy to memorize the question. The hard part is finding the right place in the conversation to ask it. As we said above, if you can't relate the question to the customer's most recent answer, you're better off not asking. If you can't work it into the story the customer is telling you, then you'll have to save it until the end of the call: "One more thing before I go…"

Note that this is one of the few times you use a closed question in the Socratic Selling process.

Chapter
10

THE
TICKING CLOCK

We have suggested that you listen for emotions and for information about the customer's needs, but there is other information you will want to gather as well—information about the customer's deadline.

As salespeople, we feel our own deadlines strongly, and naturally enough, we tend to focus on them. But the customer always has a deadline, whether she knows it or not. So you need to put aside your concern over your own deadline and find out about the customer's. Then you can help to get it into the forefront of her mind, if it's not there already. You may be able to help her avoid the consequences of missing her deadline. But a sense of urgency on her part is likely to be helpful to you as well.

The customer may face any of five types of deadlines:
- calendar
- project phase
- startup
- unspent budget
- new leadership

Calendar. Seasons, holidays, and annual events inevitably arrive year after year. Often they figure in your customer's business. Summer driving season, the fall fashion season, the carmakers' annual model introduction, winter clothing, summer clothing, construction season, allergy season, football season, flu season, back-to-school, gardening, and spring break all have well-established business implications.

As you learn more about your customer's needs, think about the changing seasons and how they might affect your customer's goals. Sometimes, customers are not even fully aware of seasonal opportunities and will be grateful to you for introducing a new level of urgency: "How does your plan relate to Daylight Saving Time?"

The way to incorporate seasonal deadlines is to study the calendar of your customer's industry and be alert to any hint of seasonal implications in the customer's conversation.

Project Phase. Any large corporate project is implemented in phases. When phases start and finish, demand for goods and services wax and wane. You can't get much help on this aspect with industry calendars. You must probe the customer's story for information about project plans and phases: "How does your goal relate to the current initiative?"

Chances are the customer is preoccupied with the current phase. It's up to you to foresee the end of this phase and the start of the next. You can be a help and a support to the customer by bringing the next phase into focus. And the next phase may well have opportunities for you—if not with this customer, then with another customer in the same company.

Startup. The startup deadline is not a very visible deadline. But when a corporate employee is given responsibility for a new undertaking, there is pressure on that employee to show that something is happening. Sometimes the pressure is overt and comes from a superior or a committee. Sometimes it is entirely internal. Either way, it's just as real.

If you are meeting with a customer about supplying products or services for some sort of new initiative, probe to find out how long ago the customer was given responsibility for it. You may be in a position to help the customer demonstrate initial results and relieve some of that pressure.

Unspent Budget. Everybody wants to save the organization money, but at some level, unspent budget represents failure. In some nonprofit organizations, this failure can be explicit. After all, when your job is spending money to help people, unspent money means you didn't do it. But even in profit-making organizations, there can be pressure to zero out the budget year, because in many organizations finishing the year with money left over means you didn't effectively project what you would need. Or it can mean that you managed to do your job with less money than was estimated, so your budget for next year will be reduced accordingly.

Probe to find out whether you could be part of the solution to the problem of unspent money. Try to get a sense of corporate cultural values: "How helpful would it be for your department to return unspent budget at the end of the year?"

New Leadership. New leadership pressure may be the most subtle of all deadline pressures. New executives are consistently advised to avoid being disruptive and to spend the first several months of their tenure studying the organization. But a new leader generally feels some pressure to make changes right away. When you think about it, changing suppliers is one of the least disruptive ways a new leader can make a change.

In addition, there are lots of new leadership situations in which avoiding disruption may not be feasible: when the new executive has been hired to turn an organization around, when an organization is in real crisis, when the new leader has already been de facto leader, when the new leader has a disruptive personal style.

You should know something about your customer's history and managers. Probe to discover how your products and services figure into the plans of any new leaders.

Now that you know the forces that create urgency for customers, use your Socratic probes to bring urgency to the surface:

- *"Why do you need to get this change made by spring?"*
- *"How does getting this done by spring affect your department?"*
- *"What would be the result of beating this spring deadline by three weeks?"*

And use active listening to learn how much pressure the deadline is giving your customer:

- *"It sounds like you feel under pressure to get this done."*
- *"I hear urgency in your voice."*
- *"I get the sense this spring deadline makes your life uncomfortable."*

Deadlines are useful to you in at least two ways: 1) they can give the customer a sense of urgency to close the deal; and 2) they can help make you a personal resource and source of support to the customer who is under pressure to meet them. So probe for them, bring them to the surface, and help the customer deal with them.

Chapter
11

PUTTING IT
ALL TOGETHER

L et's recap and see where we are at this point in the sales process:

You have used the Socratic opener to get the customer talking, and you have begun to get a view of the customer's world. By listening attentively, you have separated yourself in the customer's mind from all the salespeople who don't listen, which is to say most of them. You have used your relationship with the customer to secure an agreement for an additional meeting.

You have used a Socratic opener to get the meeting under way. You have probed the customer's story with open questions, using the interrogatories:

- What...
- Why...
- How...
- Tell me more...
- Describe...

And whenever the customer has answered one of your questions, you have listened actively by playing back, summarizing, reflecting, and taking notes. You have gathered whatever information the customer wants to share, but you have taken special care to probe areas such as the customer's:

- needs
- cognitive motivations (goals)
- learned motivations (personal associations)
- budget
- purchase authority
- deadlines

You understand the customer's needs and have created a link between those needs and your company's products and services. That link is the essence of your sales proposal, and you probably have a fairly good idea of how the customer will react to it.

You're now ready to present it to the customer.

Your Proposal

Now is not the time to get creative. Your proposal should contain nothing that the customer has not heard from you, in some form, before. In fact, your proposal will consist chiefly of what the customer has told you.

Your company may have a standard format for proposals. Make sure the proposal:

- summarizes the customer's business needs;
- takes account of the customer's goals;

- provides a compelling way to meet the customer's needs within the customer's budget;
- deals with the customer's deadlines; and
- explains your company's qualifications for delivering the solution.

Many companies like to submit hefty proposals. We have seen fat proposals filled with fancy graphics and tables, appendices, magazine and journal articles, and so on. Sometimes a fat proposal is appropriate. If you are selling custom services (like consulting or training) that will be delivered by people from your company, you may need to include a résumé or vita for each of the major people involved in the delivery.

Sometimes a fat proposal is desirable, even when there is not enough detail to really justify it. There are customers, for example, who don't like the idea of spending a large amount of money without a great deal of documentation. In such cases, a fat proposal gives the customer a feeling of security about the buying decision. This is particularly true when the product is intangible, like consulting.

Just don't think you can overawe the customer with a fat proposal. If you haven't sold the customer at this point, if you and the customer have not reached a meeting of the minds, then it's probably too late to accomplish those goals in the proposal.

Your Presentation

We have advised you to avoid making a presentation to the customer until now. But now is the time to make a presentation, based on your proposal. You could mail the proposal to the customer, but you'll make it look more important if you turn its submission into an event. And you turn your proposal into an event by making it the basis of a presentation. If the customer is amenable, ask for a meeting to present the proposal. Be sure to let the customer know it will be done as a presentation and give a time estimate for it. Keep it brief.

Even if the proposal is extensive, we recommend keeping the presentation to ten or fifteen minutes. You don't need to cover everything that's in the proposal. You'll probably be leaving a written document for the customer to review after you've gone. The presentation is mostly about the benefits of approving your proposal.

Before you launch PowerPoint and start designing slides, sketch the presentation out on paper. Structure the presentation in five parts:

- Opener
- Proposal
- Benefits
- Support
- Approval and Next Steps

Opener

The opener has a single purpose: to make the customer (or the customer's committee) feel the need your product will meet. This is the need you have come to understand as a result of questioning the customer. Your opener is a promise that your proposal will relieve the pain the organization feels as a result of the need. Remember back in chapter seven, when you were probing the customer's story, you were trying to discover three kinds of needs:

- problem (an obstacle that stands between your customer and the achievement of a goal)
- opportunity (a chance for an advantage in achieving a goal)
- weakness (a deficiency that undermines your customer's effectiveness in striving toward a goal).

Your proposal is designed to address one of these needs.

Note that failing to capitalize on an opportunity—the middle need we mentioned—can be a real cost to the customer's company. Economists call it opportunity cost. Imagine, for example, the consumer electronics company whose leaders several years ago might have said, "What's the point of making a portable MP3 player? Who wants to download music when you can have it on CDs?" Missing an opportunity that is taken by someone else is one of the deepest, most enduring types of pain to be found in business.

So, your proposal is a way to meet one of these three types of need.

Look at the three types of need again: problem, opportunity, weakness. You'll never forget what they are, if you arrange them into an acronym—Problem, Opportunity, Weakness—that spells POW!

The POW! opener gets the customer's attention and reminds her of her need. First, compose a single sentence that describes and quantifies the need:

"If _____ company misses the opportunity to put a portable MP3 player on the market, it will lose $3 million annually."

You won't actually utter this sentence as part of your proposal. You'll just keep it in your head as you compose the brief story you are going to tell that humanizes your proposal:

"At an electronics show recently, I saw a new product. Someone had taken a hard disk like the one _____ company manufactures and had put it in a pocket-sized case and attached earphones. You could download MP3 songs to it from your computer, and it held over 2,000 of them easily. And I had a vision of all the world's young people carrying around their CD collections in their pockets, playing whatever song they wanted whenever they wanted. And I realized that this is what the world has been waiting for."

Proposal

You have the customer's attention now, and he understands there's a problem, opportunity, or weakness. If you have humanized it with a story, he probably agrees with your assessment of the situation. Now it's time, while the need is uppermost in his mind, to tell him how to meet it. State your proposal.

At this stage of your presentation, your proposal is a vision of the future. Your job is to create that vision as simply as possible:

"I propose that _____ company start making a portable MP3 player in time to have it on the shelves before the next buying season."

Benefits

Up to this point, you've gotten the customer's attention by reminding her that she has a need, and you've given her a glimpse of how to meet that need. Now it's time to walk her over the bridge to the informational part of your presentation. That bridge is the benefit of adopting your proposal.

To show your customer that the solution you're about to propose is worth the cost, you explain the benefits—how the solution will make his life better.

These benefits are specific, and they specifically apply to the customer (or the members of the customer's committee). Remember, we are talking about a particular impact on their lives. Will it:

- Let them get their work done quicker?
- Make their jobs more secure?
- Make their vacations longer?
- Make them more prestigious or powerful?

Figure out two benefits of the solution you're proposing. State the strongest benefit second, where it will be more prominent. The description of a benefit, incidentally, nearly always includes some form of the word "you."

When you state a benefit, imagine a specific, quantifiable outcome you can use to make it real. Don't say, "This will let you get your work done quicker." Say, "This will let you go home at 4:00 each day." Don't say, "This will make your company more prestigious." Say, "This will make people pause to emphasize your company's name when they speak it."

In other words, create a mental picture for the customer of what her life will be like after the sale.

Support

At this point, the customer should be sympathetic to your proposal. Since it is based on needs he has expressed to you, he probably wants to adopt it. After all, he has a need, he has glimpsed a way to meet it, and now he has seen the benefit to his life of adopting it. Now you deal with whatever remaining skepticism he might have by offering evidence to support your proposal.

Evidence comes in five forms:
* data
* expertise
* cases
* image
* story

The first, data, is the one used most often in presentations. Data are the statistics and facts that have put so many of us to sleep in the course of someone else's presentation. You need to remember that data is one type of evidence among many, and it's not the most effective type. Pull all your data together, and then choose a few of your most powerful points to present. Keep the rest for the written proposal.

The second type of evidence, expertise, is the opinion of someone your customer will accept as an authority on the subject—an expert, in other words. Expert opinion is valuable if you have it. That's one of the reasons they use it in court during trials.

The third type of evidence, cases, is most useful when you have examples that are close to the experience of your customer or particularly meaningful to her. Cases or examples are useful because they show real world applications.

The fourth type of evidence, image, is used to relate your proposal to something familiar. Image is an explanatory form of evidence; it doesn't prove anything. To say that the company's new MP3 player is like a Walkman™ but never needs a tape or disc change, is just a way to help the customer visualize it.

The fifth type of evidence, story, is something from your personal experience. It may not readily prove your contentions, but it brings them to life.

The five types of evidence—Data, Expertise, Cases, Image, Story—help your audience come to a decision about your recommendation, and they form an acronym: DECISion.

Evidence will probably be the largest single section of your presentation. You can be a little more expansive with it than you are with the other sections. But don't make the mistake of thinking you can overwhelm the customer with evidence and wear down his resistance. You may indeed be able to wear him down, but bored people are rarely excited enough to close.

Action

The last step before questions and answers is to ask the customer to take the first step toward buying. Now is the time to provide a deadline. But note that it is always the customer's deadline, not yours. If you try to impose your own deadline, such as "I can only hold this price for 24 hours," you're using a pressure close, and that could undo all your work up to now.

You have information about the customer's deadline. Remember the previous chapter in which we looked at calendar, project phase, startup, remaining budget, and new leadership. Incorporate what you learned about the customer's deadline into your call to action:

- "To take advantage of the next buying season, I recommend making a decision within 10 days."

- "To be ready for the next stage of the rollout, I recommend making a commitment by Monday."
- "To get the project launched as quickly as possible, I recommend a decision before the end of the week."
- "To make sure the project is on this year's budget, we need to have the paperwork underway by the end of the month, and I recommend a decision within seven days."
- "To show that the new management is serious about change, I recommend a commitment within 10 days."

You will be leaving the written proposal with the customer, who will no doubt want to study it before making the commitment. Because you're leaving a written proposal, we recommend keeping this presentation brief. Unless the proposal is highly complex, the customer will probably be grateful if you keep the presentation to 10 or 15 minutes.

Having sketched out this presentation on paper, it's okay now to open PowerPoint and create the slides that will support it.

Chapter 12

Making Use of Objections

Objections can occur at almost any point in the sales process, but they are most likely to occur as you near the close and the customer can feel the hot breath of commitment on his neck. No matter how compelling your proposal, no matter how much the customer trusts you, no matter how strong the customer's need for your solution, buying from you is still a risk. And the customer may need support to take the risk.

What Is an Objection?

An objection is a reason the customer gives for not signing the order now. Anybody who's ever sold anything can recite dozens of them:

- *"It's too expensive."*
- *"The warranty isn't long enough."*
- *"I can't wait 30 days for delivery."*
- *"I don't like the blue."*

The more specific the objection, the less likely it is to be a deal breaker—if the salesperson knows how to deal with objections. When the customer makes a specific objection, it means she is already interacting with the product in her mind. If the customer is imagining what life would be like with the product, you're well on your way to closing. The important thing to remember is that an objection is not a rejection. A customer would not raise an objection if she weren't engaged.

A customer's objection can convey more than it may seem to at first. It can be:

- a request for more information;
- an expression of desire;
- a plea for support in assuming the risk of purchasing;
- a request to slow the sales process;
- a test of your firmness;
- a set-up for a negotiating position; or
- exactly what it purports to be.

This list is suggestive, not exhaustive. It would be impossible to list everything an objection could be. How, then, do you find out what an objection really represents so you can deal with it? Socratically.

Deal with an Objection Socratically

First, never object to an objection. That's part of agenda-based selling, and it does nothing to further the sale. If a customer says, "I don't like blue," and you reply by saying, "Blue's a great color," you're being dismissive.

That may be a silly example, but it's all too easy to be dismissive of customer concerns:

> *Customer: "This contract is too expensive."*
> *Salesperson: "It's much more cost-effective than the one being offered by our competitor."*
> *Customer: "I still think it's overpriced."*
> *Salesperson: "The included support package alone is worth the cost of the contract."*

A conversation like the one above sounds more businesslike than the one about whether the customer dislikes the color blue, but the salesperson is being just as dismissive. The salesperson isn't arguing with the customer, but she's not dealing with the concern, either.

Second, although we said it's possible for an objection to be just what it purports to be, you should never take it at face value. Socratic Selling offers you a way to find out more about it.

No matter what the objection is, you should repeat it to show the customer you've heard it, then probe to see what's behind it with a simple question:

> *"Why do you say that?"*

Here's the conversation from above, this time with a Socratic salesperson:

> *Customer: "This contract is too expensive."*
> *Salesperson: "Expensive. Why do you say that?"*
> *Customer: "I can't budget $10,000 up front."*

This salesperson now has something to work with. It's not the overall expense that concerns the customer. It's the up-front payment.

The salesperson who doesn't probe an objection will never learn if it's more than it appears to be. You may have to probe even further:

> *Customer:* "*This contract is too expensive.*"
> *Salesperson:* "*Expensive. Why do you say that?*"
> *Customer:* "*I can't budget $10,000 up front.*"
> *Salesperson:* "*I hear you saying $10,000 is too large for an up-front payment. How much do you usually budget for an up-front payment on this kind of contract?*"
> *Customer:* "*Our current provider starts the service for $7,500.*"

Now the salesperson really knows what "too expensive" means. It means more than the competitor charges for the up-front payment. The salesperson may not be in a position to make a price adjustment but may be in a position to change the payment terms. Perhaps the customer would be willing to make the initial payment in two $5,000 payments. Or there may be some other creative way to deal with it. The point is that you must probe any objection to find out what the customer really means.

Protect Your Work

Regardless of what the objection really means or represents, once it has gotten loose into the dialogue, it can damage all the work you've done to this point. If the customer doesn't feel that you are dealing with it, it becomes not just an objection, but an objection that isn't getting any attention. And that can damage your relationship.

But you shouldn't jump in to resolve it too quickly, either. You might wind up making a concession of some sort to resolve the objection, only to find more objections, which you will then make concessions to resolve, until you've conceded away the sale's profitability. And you should not overlook the possibility that if you immediately resolve the customer's objection, the customer could see this as a "win," which itself encourages more objections.

You have done a great deal of work at this point to understand the customer, create a relationship with him, and link his need to your product. You need to protect this work, and you need to make sure there aren't other issues. You accomplish these two things by isolating the objection:

> *"If we could resolve this up-front payment issue, and I know we haven't yet, but if we could, is there anything else standing in the way of our doing business?"*

Once you've made sure there's nothing else standing in the way of doing business, you can resolve the objection:

"How about this idea? If you agree to start in October, we defer half the up-front payment until March. That saves you $2,500 over your previous arrangement and lets you put half the up-front payment on next year's budget. And it still gives you the included support package. How does that sound?"

Notice how the resolution is packaged. The salesperson offers it as an idea, states it simply, follows it immediately with a summary of benefits, and then asks for the customer's reaction.

Now you have isolated and resolved the objection. The customer has already agreed there is nothing left to stand in the way of doing business. It may be time to ask for the order.

Chapter
13

THE
SOCRATIC CLOSING

Most salespeople are taught to look for "buying signals" from the customer. As soon as you see the signal, you're supposed to attempt a close. We have seen sales training programs that insist you are supposed to attempt a close at every customer meeting.

What are these buying signals? A buying signal is anything you can detect as a positive change in the customer's attitude toward the product. If the customer begins to physically handle the product, for example, many salespeople interpret that as a buying signal. If she asks to test it or try it out; if she asks about price, delivery times, or terms; if she asks for references; if she asks about buying incentives; these are all signs that the customer has begun to interact with the product. Many sales training programs advise the salesperson to attempt a trial close whenever he sees such signals.

In Socratic Selling, on the other hand, you communicate with the customer on a more rational level. You don't rely on strange, involuntary signs to gauge the customer's inner state. You have, in fact, probed the customer's inner state and relayed it back to him in the form of your proposal.

The close is not going to be a dramatic moment of decision. It is going to be the natural result of your having determined the customer's need and offered a solution to meet that need.

How Not to Close

In this book, we have repeatedly criticized the trial close:

> *"If I were able to show you right now a way you could _____ without changing _____, would we have a basis for doing business?"*

But there are other pressure closes that are common in agenda-based selling, starting with the classic car dealer's line, "What would it take to put you in this car today?" Some of the others include:

- *"What if I gave you _____. Would you buy right now?"*
- *"If you sign the contract within the next fifteen minutes, I can give you a 10 percent discount."*
- *"Will that be cash or charge?"*
- *"Do you know Bill Gates? He just ordered a dozen of these."*
- *"Do you want the extended service or the pro package?"*

Anything that tries to take the decision out of the customer's hands is a pressure close, as is anything that tries to fool the customer into thinking she's making a decision on some other matter. You can see that time pressure is a favorite.

How to Close

After you have responded to all the customer's objections and the customer has agreed that your responses are workable and will meet his needs, it's time to summarize what you and the customer have accomplished.

Restate the customer's need, the main elements of your proposal, and any agreements you have made to handle objections. Then ask for the customer's agreement on the summary:

"Does that sound right to you?"

Your summary has laid out the basis for the sale. When the customer agrees to the accuracy of the summary, the logical next step is to ask for the order. Use a closed question:

- *"Are we ready to move forward?"*
- *"Do we have a deal?"*
- *"Are you ready to sign? If so, I can put it in the system for delivery next week."*

It's no coincidence that this chapter on closing is the shortest one in the book. In Socratic Selling, the close is both simple and brief.

Chapter
14

NEGOTIATING
SOCRATICALLY

In 1815, the great European powers—England, Austria, Russia, and Prussia—had united to defeat Napoleon. They claimed the right to redraw the map of Europe and they met at the Congress of Vienna to do just that.

France, as the defeated enemy, had no influence in the Congress and did not even have the right to sit at the negotiating table. But the allies allowed King Louis XVIII, who had been restored to the French throne after Napoleon's abdication, to send a representative. The king sent his foreign minister, Talleyrand, who used the occasion to accomplish the greatest negotiation in history.

The year before, in their haste to make peace with France, the allied powers had agreed to a treaty that was comparatively generous. It let France keep its 1792 boundaries (which included some early revolutionary conquests), required it to pay no indemnity, and withdrew foreign troops from its soil right away.

But the allied powers were not bound to continue these arrangements, and the Congress of Vienna was held in part to revisit them. For millennia, European states had observed a tradition of carving up and bankrupting defeated countries.

Talleyrand came to Vienna with the goal of preserving the current treaty and preventing any punishment of France for the revolutionary wars or Napoleon. Imagine how little he had to put on the table. He represented a country that was defeated and that had expended a generation of young men waging wars of conquest. Its treasury was depleted, its army was reduced, and its prestige was gone. Far worse than being an object of contempt, it was a focus of European fears, for the continent's kings and princes had seen the kind of havoc it could wreak. In the end, France had nothing the great powers wanted. To the extent they were united on any question, it was that France should be punished for what it had done.

And yet, when Talleyrand finally returned from Vienna, he brought to his king not only the generous terms of the Treaty of Paris but recognition that France was a great power and entitled to engage other nations as an equal. The Congress of Vienna, whatever else may be said about it, ushered in the longest period of European peace ever known.

How did Talleyrand accomplish this remarkable feat? He managed to get himself an invitation to a meeting of the ambassadors of the four allied powers. At the meeting, he listened carefully to the speeches that were made. Prince von Hardenberg of Prussia, in the course of his speech, mentioned the allied powers.

Here is Talleyrand's account of his own remarks:

I repeated with some astonishment and even
warmth, the word *allied powers…"allied,"* I said,
"and against whom? It is no longer Napoleon—he
is on the isle of Elba…it is no longer against
France; for peace has been made…it is surely not
against the King of France; he is a guarantee of
the duration of that peace. Gentlemen, let us
speak frankly; if there are still *allied powers,* I am
one too many here. And nevertheless if I were not
here, I should decidedly be missed. Gentlemen, I
am perhaps the only one who asks nothing…I
want nothing, I repeat it, but I bring you a great
deal. The presence of a minister of Louis XVIII
consecrates here the principle upon which all
social order rests. The first need of Europe is to
banish for ever the opinion that right can be
acquired by conquest alone, and to cause the
revival of that sacred principle of legitimacy from
which all order and stability spring." (Raphael
Ledos de Beaufort, trans., *Memoirs of the Prince de
Talleyrand, vol. 2* [G. P. Putnam's Sons, 1891;
New York: AMS Press Inc., 1973], 203)

It may be a little wordy for modern tastes, but this
little speech focuses brilliantly on the primary interests
of the great powers. They wanted peace and stability,
and they wanted a repudiation of revolution and conquest. What Talleyrand is saying is that the restored King
Louis XVIII, who is one of their own, is himself the

repudiation of revolution and conquest they desire. The clear implication, of course, which he wisely left out of the speech, is that if the great powers punish France, they would be the revolutionaries and they would be the ones engaging in conquest. Needless to say, the negotiations went his way after that.

There are two lessons here. The first is that you negotiate successfully by looking to the interests of the other party (without ever forgetting your own!). The second is that for a creative and empathetic mind, no negotiation is ever hopeless.

Your "Get/Give" List

At some point, the customer has agreed to your proposal and it's time to decide on the terms of the sale. For many customers, that means it's time to start making amendments to what you are already agreed to. You're in the same position as Talleyrand. You have an agreement, but the other party wants concessions in order to honor it.

You already have some experience with what comes next, from when you handled the customer's objections. There, you looked for the real issue, isolated it, and suggested a creative way to solve it. You will be drawing on that ability again.

But sometimes there will be issues that you cannot solve creatively, and you must decide whether to make concessions.

Our advice is, Do not make concessions.

Here's why we say that. Let's say the customer demands that you lower the price. Many salespeople have no authority over price, but let's say you do. If you make a price concession, the customer may assume that your product was overpriced to begin with. This reduces her confidence in you. Suddenly, you look as if you haven't been straight with her on price. Pretty soon, she's questioning other parts of the agreement, endangering the sale.

What can you do if you won't make concessions? Trade. You can trade without endangering the relationship you have built.

What do you have to trade? If Talleyrand could find something to trade in Vienna, surely you can find something to trade in your sale. Some things that may be under your control:

- price
- timing of delivery
- timing of payments
- extra resources
- product model
- service and support
- related supplies and ancillary products

If, for example, the customer demands a reduction in price that you can't make, perhaps you can offer an extension on the service period that may mean as much financially to the customer. Perhaps you can throw in some supplies, speed up delivery, or give the customer access to resources, such as a database or an important person at your company.

There are also items of value the customer may control that you might be willing to take in exchange for something the customer wants: referrals to other people in the customer's company, the sale of ancillary products, a later delivery deadline, or a longer commitment.

Before you begin negotiating, you need to know what you'd like to get and what you can afford to give. Establish a maximum for each. You need to know in advance what you are willing to walk away from. Otherwise, you may pass that point in the heat of negotiations and end up agreeing to a deal that will cost more than you make on it.

Once you have the get/give list, you can use it to set the limits of your trades.

The Format for a Trade

Negotiating requires a lot of thinking on one's feet, both on your side and the customer's. In order to build in the time for this thinking and slow down the pace of the negotiation, we recommend a specific format for responses and counteroffers:

1. Play back the customer request.
2. Explain why the request exceeds your limits.
3. Invite the customer to respond to a counteroffer.
4. Present the counteroffer, with benefits.

Each of the four parts is important, and it's there for a reason.

Play back the customer request. This is active listening again. You need to make sure you've heard the customer's request properly, and you need to show the customer you are listening. In addition, playing back can give you more time for thinking if you need it:

> *"Let me be sure I'm clear on what you're asking for. You're saying you need it in 60 days instead of the normal 90-day delivery time, because by the time you get your people trained, it would be 120 days until you could use it. Do I have that correct?"*

Explain why the request exceeds your limits. Unlike some negotiation strategies, Socratic negotiating is not secretive. You're not trying to hide the reasons for your position from the customer. You want the customer to have the information, partly so she will understand why she's not getting what she wants, and partly so she has more information to use in proposing solutions on her side:

> *"I want to explain to you why that's more than we can do.*
>
> *Our plant is running at full capacity on a 90-day production cycle. As you know, this product is customized to your needs. We need 90 days to manufacture it."*

Invite the customer to respond to a counteroffer. Don't just throw out a counteroffer. Let the customer know you're going to suggest something else and pose it as a discussion point. This helps to ensure you're continuing two-way communication:

> *"Would you like to discuss an idea that might solve this problem?"*

Present the counteroffer, with benefits. In the final step, you describe your proposed solution, couched in terms of "If you/then I." Here is how it looks:

> *"If you would agree to a 90-day delivery, then I would arrange for your people to train at our plant for 30 days before delivery, so you could be up to speed when the equipment arrives and be using it productively in 90 days instead of 120."*

You have made this counteroffer as a subject for discussion. The customer may agree, may criticize it, or may present a counter-counteroffer. No matter what the outcome, however, you're still talking, you haven't conceded anything you couldn't afford to concede, and the sale is still alive.

Chapter
15

PLANNING THE SALES CALL

We have described the elements of Socratic Selling from the first customer meeting onward. In fact, however, the sales call begins long before you meet with the customer. Your listening and your probes will be far more effective if they are based on some preliminary knowledge.

The most professional of sales professionals plan meticulously for sales calls. It may seem strange that we put the chapter on planning at the end, but we did that to give listening and questioning the top billing they deserve. Also, planning for sales calls is pretty much the same no matter what kind of selling you do, Socratic or not.

You may be able to find more comprehensive sources of information on sales-call planning, but we wanted to discuss it at some length here because planning is critical to Socratic Selling. Planning gives you the framework for your listening and your probes during the call.

The preliminary knowledge you need for your plan is of three types:
- knowledge of the customer
- knowledge of the customer's company
- knowledge of the customer's industry

Customer. First of all, find out everything you can about the customer. Google him. Has he written articles? Does he maintain a blog? A podcast? Does he participate in web forums? Does the company website contain a bio on him? Speeches he's given? Press releases about him?

Here are some of the things you would like to know about the customer before you meet with him:
- job title/role in the company
- apparent level of buying authority
- goals for the meeting with you
- business history with your company

In addition, you should have some idea of why he agreed to meet with you.

You may not be able to find the information you need on the web. You can try the company's annual report, if the customer is high enough in the structure. There may even be other people, such as assistants and administrative staff, who could give you information about the customer. Finding such people is more difficult than it once was. But if you can find someone to talk to, be up front about your need for information: "I'm meeting with her next week, and I want to prepare for the meeting." Ask only for public information and use active listening techniques to draw out the person you interview.

Company. Most companies have websites, and they can be treasure troves for researchers. In addition to getting an overall feel for what the company is about, look especially for links called "who we are" and "press room." "Who we are" usually provides history and often gives profiles of the top executives. "Press room" usually has press releases, speeches by the company's executives, and news, often including articles published about the company or its products.

You should also Google the company the same way you did your customer. Often you can find reviews of its products, customer complaints about it, and speculations about its strategy.

If you can get the company's annual report, that will give you a good idea of how the company's management team wants it to be perceived, and the report may offer more information than you will find on the website. In addition, if it's a public company, it is required to file 10-K reports annually. 10-Ks are a lot less colorful than your average annual report, but they include stuff you won't find in a regular annual report, such as events that could materially affect the company's business. Use the EDGAR database of the Securities and Exchange Commission to locate 10-Ks. You can find it at www.sec.gov/edgar/searchedgar/webusers.htm.

Your company may subscribe to other Internet sources of company information: LexisNexis, Hoover's,

The Wall Street Journal, Dun & Bradstreet, Standard & Poor's, and so on.

Here are some of the things you want to know about the company:

- key trends
- competitive position
- strengths/weaknesses
- threats/opportunities
- "public face" (executive speeches, interviews, etc.)
- major decisions made or currently being faced
- primary market strategy, product differentiation
- recent expansions or reductions
- reception of latest product
- nature of customer population

Industry. Some of the sources you examined for information about the company will also have insights about its industry. There are also industry magazines and websites, general business magazines, the newspaper in the company's "home town," and industry associations. All these are fairly easily found on the web. Start with a Google search on the term "____ industry," where the blank is the appropriate name of your company's industry. If you find a website for an industry association, they often have lots of links, including provider directories (which can help you get an idea about your customer's competitors).

Here are some of the things you want to know about the customer's industry:

- profile (mature, emerging, evolving)

- level of competition among industry players
- activities of the major competitors
- industry strengths/weaknesses
- industry threats/opportunities
- distribution of market share and trends
- pending legislation that may affect the industry
- influential mergers and acquisitions
- level of competitor aggression, recent moves
- the use being made of your product by players in the industry, particularly your customer's competitors

Planning the Meeting

Now that you are something of an expert on the customer, her company, and her industry, you need to plan a strategy for the meeting. This strategy has two parts: what you want to discover during the meeting and what you want to achieve in it.

Discovery. No matter how much information you find on the customer, company, and industry, you really can't know a customer well until you sit in her office and talk with her. One of your goals for the sales meeting should be to acquire information you need to understand the customer and her needs. Here are some of the things you want to learn by listening and probing:

- What value does the customer's business put on your product?
- What's the company's decision-making process for buying a product like yours?

- What's the range of the budget?
- How urgent is the need? When do they want it?
- How will they implement the decision to buy?
- Which of your competitors will they be looking at?
- What is their current business relationship with your competitor(s)?
- Which of your competitors have they talked to?
- How does the customer perceive your company?
- Whom else in the company should you speak with?

Outcomes. In the best of all possible worlds, the customer buys your product the first time you meet with him. We rarely find ourselves in the best of all possible worlds, so you need to establish interim goals that will help you through the multi-meeting sales process. You may as well put a sale at the top of your list of outcomes you are seeking:

- a sale
- referral inside or outside the company
- agreement to advance you to a committee or the next level
- agreement to provide information
- agreement to try a sample
- agreement to respond to further information you'll provide
- agreement to consider a formal proposal
- agreement to advance your idea within the company
- agreement to a follow-up meeting
- agreement to see a product demo

With your background information, your goals for what you want to learn, and your goals for what you want to achieve, you'll be ready to make the best use of the first meeting.

Epilogue:

Today, 2,400 years after his death, Socrates still reigns as one of the most influential philosophers who ever lived—a significant accomplishment for a man who never wrote anything for posterity.

It's quite possible that serious scholars of Socrates would be aghast at the use we have made of him as an icon for Socratic Selling. Most scholars, when they think about selling at all, imagine it in terms of white shoes, plaid sport coats, insincere smiles, and the line, "What do I have to do to put you in this car today?"

But selling has that reputation because sellers have traditionally been too busy selling to look at their work philosophically. In fact, selling is a profoundly philosophical activity, and it has only gained its unsavory reputation as a result of the efforts of those who don't approach it that way.

If some people think it is wrong to appropriate Socrates' name and values for a selling program, it's not because there's anything in Socrates' philosophy that disapproves of selling. It's because of the reputation that hard-driving, oblivious salespeople have given the activity. There is nothing inherently selfish, manipulative, or exploitive in selling. There just happen to have been some selfish, manipulative, exploitive people doing it— and some good people, who, because of their lack of sound sales training, have accidentally found themselves selling in selfish, manipulative, and exploitive ways.

Socratic Selling skills exist to help salespeople train themselves out of selfishness and manipulation, for ultimately those are neither successful nor career-enhancing activities.

The commitment of the Socratic salesperson, like that of Socrates himself, is to the welfare of others. It's true that Socrates took this commitment as far as it could possibly go. Few of us would be willing to drink ground up hemlock as part of the sales transaction. But those who have joined the Socratic Selling fraternity have done so because this method puts the customer, rather than the seller, at the center of the selling process.

We wish you success and prosperity in your selling career, but more than that, we wish you a Socratic view of life and the opportunity to serve others. Socrates, we assure you, would have approved.

About
Communispond

Communispond was founded in 1969 to teach business professionals to make effective presentations. Presentations often turn out to be career-making moments for people, but before Communispond, few organizations routinely trained their employees for them.

The firm soon found itself in great demand for preparing executives, sales professionals, celebrities, and political candidates for high-stakes communications events.

In training people to make sales presentations, Communispond realized early in its history that most sales professionals don't know how to listen. So the firm stepped to the other side of the platform to teach listening skills, developing its famous Socratic Selling Skills.

Communispond's clients demanded the firm develop more and more programs for different communication disciplines.

Today, Communispond offers training and coaching in virtually every type of business communication: business writing, interviewing, being interviewed, listening, webinar facilitation, sales, customer service, negotiating, coaching, and presentation skills. It offers training, coaching, and consulting—all rigorously behavior-based.

Sales and Customer Relations remain one of Communispond's strongest specialties, with programs in

- Selling by Phone
- Socratic Selling Skills
- Sales Presentation Skills
- Business Negotiating Skills
- Coaching for Improved Sales Performance
- Hiring the Right Salesperson
- Write to Sell
- Call Centers-Solving Customers' Problems

Communispond's clients include more than 350 of the Fortune 500. Its "graduates" number more than 500,000 people, many of them industry leaders from all over the world.

C O M M U N I S P O N D™

Communispond
52 Vanderbilt Avenue
New York, NY 10017
800-529-5925
www.communispond.com